Patron-Driven Acquisitions

For over a decade, some academic libraries have been purchasing, rather than borrowing, recently published books requested by their patrons through interlibrary loan. These books had one circulation guaranteed and so appealed to librarians who were concerned about the large percentage of books selected by librarians but never checked out. Assessments of these patron-driven acquisitions projects indicate that patrons select quality books that in many cases are cross disciplinary and cover emerging areas of scholarly interest. The projects described in this book present a powerful argument for involving patrons in the book selection process.

This book looks at patron-driven acquisitions for printed books at Purdue University, the University of Nebraska-Lincoln, and the University of Illinois. It also explores new programs that allow patrons to select e-books or to participate in other innovative ways in building the library collections.

This book was previously published as a special issue of *Collection Management*.

Judith M. Nixon is currently the College of Education Librarian and responsible for building the education collection. Past positions at Purdue have involved her in collection development efforts in subjects as varied as nutrition and management. Her interest in patron-driven acquisitions comes from her focus on providing the best services to users.

Robert S. Freeman is Reference and Foreign Languages & Literatures Librarian for the Purdue University Libraries. He is responsible for collection development in several foreign languages and literatures, as well as in linguistics, comparative literature, classical studies, Asian studies, and music. His research interests include library history and publishing history.

Suzanne M. Ward is Head, Collection Management for the Purdue University Libraries. In her former position at Purdue as Head, Access Services, she was an early implementer of the interlibrary loan book purchasing model and was active in the resource sharing arena. Her current interests include analyzing low use print material for potential de-selection.

Patron-Driven Acquisitions
Current Successes and Future Directions

Edited by
Judith M. Nixon, Robert S. Freeman, and Suzanne M. Ward

Routledge
Taylor & Francis Group

LONDON AND NEW YORK

First published 2011
by Routledge
2 Park Square, Milton Park, Abingdon, Oxon, OX14 4RN

Simultaneously published in the USA and Canada
by Routledge
711 Third Avenue, New York, NY 10017

Routledge is an imprint of the Taylor & Francis Group, an informa business

This book is a reproduction of *Collection Management*, vol. 35, issue 3-4. The Publisher requests to those authors who may be citing this book to state, also, the bibliographical details of the special issue on which the book was based.

Typeset in Garamond by Taylor & Francis Books

British Library Cataloguing in Publication Data
A catalogue record for this book is available from the British Library

ISBN13: 978-0-415-61870-0

Disclaimer
The publisher would like to make readers aware that the chapters in this book are referred to as articles as they had been in the special issue. The publisher accepts responsibility for any inconsistencies that may have arisen in the course of preparing this volume for print.

Erratum
Since the original special issue was published, Anne C. Barnhart (author of chapter 12) has changed affiliation and is now at the University of Georgia, Carrollton, Georgia.

Contents

CONTENTS

Innovative Services/New Directions

An Introduction
and Literature Review

JUDITH M. NIXON, ROBERT S. FREEMAN,
and SUZANNE M. WARD
Purdue University, West Lafayette, Indiana

Libraries exist for their users, so librarians take user needs into consideration when building collections. In the past, this consideration took many forms. Past use suggested that more books of a similar nature would receive future use. The librarians' knowledge about a particular user community's interest in certain topics drove other choices; a public library collection in a rural area would include books on some topics unlikely to interest urban dwellers, for example. Academic libraries would emphasize subjects taught or researched at the institution. A small liberal arts college's collection would focus on some different subject areas than a polytechnic institution. A museum library might buy few titles outside the field of the fine and decorative arts. Traditionally, librarians relied on book reviews, publisher reputation, and professional intuition to guide them in the selection of books for their patrons. While most librarians seriously considered users' requests for specific titles if they met the library's collection development policies, in general librarians selected the vast majority of titles. To borrow a term from industry, librarians historically built collections on the "just in case" inventory model.

Starting in the late 1970s, the results of several studies showed that users in major academic library collections checked out an astonishingly low percentage of these largely librarian-selected books (Kent 1979). One frequently cited study revealed that 20% of the collection receives 80% of the use (Trueswell 1969). These studies suggested that the traditional model of librarian-selected titles does not serve users, at least not at academic institutions, as well as librarians expected. At the same time, skyrocketing interlibrary loan (ILL) figures from the Association of Research Libraries member libraries also indicated that local collections do not meet needs adequately (Libraries 2009, 9). Certainly some of the ILL traffic is for unusual, obscure, or specialized titles needed for advanced research, but a large number of requests are for "ordinary" titles that normal collection development practices did not predict would be needed.

Librarians have long recognized the need to base collection development decisions on analysis (Blake and Schleper 2005; Carrigan 1996; Knievel et al. 2006; Mortimore 2006; Ruppel 2006). Some librarians have tried analyzing filled ILL transactions to select or predict subject areas that should be emphasized in the collection (Aguilar 1986; Byrd et al. 1982; Livingston and Mays 2004; New and Ott 1974; Roberts and Cameron 1984; Wender 1969; Wood and Bower 1969). This approach misses the moment of need, however, and at best results in buying books only after the library has already expended resources borrowing titles one or more times. ILL transactions are expensive. Even if many of a particular library's supplying partners are part of a mutually cooperative consortium that does not assess per-loan charges among members, there is a cost involved for ILL transactions.

By the early 2000s, more and more libraries explored a new approach that resembled industry's "just in time" inventory model. When patrons requested books through ILL, libraries began buying the titles if they met certain preestablished criteria generally focused on variables such as price, delivery time, and appropriate content. After initial use by the requesting ILL patrons, the books (and, later, media titles) were added to the regular library collection. Librarians conducting subsequent use studies on these titles discovered surprisingly high circulation figures for these patron-selected titles when compared with similar traditionally acquired titles, even considering that at least some of the subsequent use was probably by the same patrons who placed the initial requests (Anderson et al. 2002; Perdue and Van Fleet 1999). In one study, selectors' reviews of patron-selected titles agreed that the vast majority of them were appropriate for the collection (Anderson et al. 2002).

From today's perspective, the ease and effectiveness of what is now commonly called patron-driven acquisitions, or user-initiated collection development, seem so obvious. What better way to build at least a portion of the collection than by letting the users' directly expressed needs guide the expenditure of scarce collection development funds? Not only are the requesting patrons' needs satisfied, but also it is highly likely that those books will interest other patrons in the future.

Obvious as the practice seems today, the early implementers encountered snags. For example, Bucknell College's initial venture in 1990 was only partially successful because some book orders were delayed over difficulties such as being out of print or requiring prepayment (Perdue and Van Fleet 1999). The concept was not fully realizable until the rise of the online booksellers, when library staff could quickly and easily check price and in-stock status with suppliers committed to rapid fulfillment.

Librarians began reporting the buy versus borrow programs at their individual libraries (selected examples: Ward 2002; Clendenning 2001; Brug and MacWaters 2004; Foss 2007). While these libraries' purchase criteria considered the same variables, those variables often had very different values. For example, some libraries circulated the book to the ILL patron before cataloging it; others rush-cataloged the incoming books. Some libraries' pilot programs began with very modest funding; others were sufficiently funded to buy all the books that met the criteria. Maximum cost per book varied. Some libraries also bought books from the used book market or from international booksellers; others did not. Some libraries reviewed all new ILL loan requests for possible purchase; others only examined titles that had failed in the first borrowing attempt through traditional ILL channels. One beauty of the model is that each library can set the parameters that suit it best.

By 2003, *Library Journal* published an article about "purchase on demand" (Hulsey 2003), and in 2004 a librarian at the University of Hong Kong offered an international perspective (Chan 2004). The literature also began to acknowledge the necessary partnerships between library units or functions that formerly had had little interaction: ILL with acquisitions and/or with collection development (Ward et al. 2003). By today, most people reviewing the literature will be convinced that the patron-driven acquisitions model has proved itself on a number of levels, including cost-effective collection development; user satisfaction; high subsequent circulation; and flexibility in meeting local constraints for price, content, and processing. It is no longer a revolutionary concept, but one that is accepted as routine in many sizes and types of libraries.

Patron-driven acquisition is also a concept that easily and naturally moves beyond the print and media arenas into electronic books. It is now just about as easy to order an individual e-book title from a book jobber's list as it is to choose a print title from an online bookseller's site. By adding the e-book to the catalog and sending the patron an e-mail with the link, the library fulfills the request in a matter of hours instead of days, with every expectation that the patron-selected e-book will receive more future use by other patrons than some librarian-selected ones. On this front, the vendors are so convinced of the model's success that several of them have developed patron-driven acquisition versions of their lists. The library loads the records, possibly preselected or refined in some way by the librarians, into its online public access catalog. There, patrons find e-book records that look the same as any other e-book records. After a certain number of browses or after a certain amount of time viewing each book, the library pays for the title and adds it permanently to the collection. Librarians were initially cautious of adding this service, concerned that the ease of selecting an e-book would lead to runaway expenses. Recent research by Jason Price and John McDonald, however, indicates that these fears may be exaggerated (Price and McDonald 2009). During this time of transition between print and electronic (however long it lasts), many libraries may chose to maintain patron-driven acquisition programs in both formats to satisfy patrons who have compelling needs to consult either version.

The editors are three of the six authors who wrote "Buy, Don't Borrow: Bibliographers' Analysis of Academic Library Collection Development Through Interlibrary Loan Requests" for *Collection Management* (Anderson et al. 2002). Realizing that the program had nearly reached its tenth anniversary, the six authors met in 2009 to discuss conducting the same analysis on 10 years of data that had been conducted on the initial two years of data. Would the results be similar? Would a program that had appeared promising after its first two years still be fulfilling its promise? Would some earlier hints at unexpected results, such as high subsequent circulation and strong evidence of interdisciplinary use, show development over a decade? While discussing the scope of the new article, however, it quickly became clear that far more analysis could be done with a decade of data than had been possible after only two years. For example, all the patron-driven acquisition titles could be compared with all the normally acquired books over 10 years to examine circulation patterns. Then a colleague in one of the Purdue University science libraries expressed an interest in analyzing the science and technology books. Several of us wanted to ponder the effect of this shift toward patron-driven acquisitions and its effect on collection development librarians' roles. With four article ideas already in the works, the editors were pleased when Faye Chadwell, *Collection Management* editor, accepted their proposal for a special issue about patron-driven acquisitions.

In fall 2009, the editors sent a call for papers to over 100 library Listservs around the world. They received 30 paper proposals. The editors selected papers that fell into three major categories: those that best represented practice in the traditional print-based patron-driven acquisition programs based on ILL requests; those describing the experiences of early implementers of e-book patron-driven acquisition programs; and those from librarians with truly innovative concepts for involving patrons in the collection development process. Despite the wide distribution of the call for papers, no proposals came from public libraries or from special libraries. The few proposals from international libraries were not among those finally selected. Although the resulting articles mainly report patron-driven acquisitions activities at large American academic libraries, the editors hope that many of the ideas and practices will be in some way adaptable to other sizes, types, and locations of libraries.

ACKNOWLEDGEMENTS

The editors are grateful to Tim Bowersox, MaryLou Epp, Kathleen Carlisle Fountain, Linda Frederiksen, Jeanne Harrell, Marsha J. Hamilton, Dracine Hodges, Anita M. Kreps, Joyce C. Melvin, Cyril Oberlander, Carmelita Pickett,

Kate Pitcher, Cyndi Preston, Leslie J. Reynolds, Jane Smith, Mark Sullivan, Sandra Tucker, David C. Tyler, Wyoma vanDuinkerken, and Yang Xu for their contributions to the reference list.

E. Stewart Saunders made valuable contributions to this issue by offering suggestions for articles involving statistics.

REFERENCES

Aguilar, William. 1986. The application of relative use and interlibrary demand in collection development. *Collection Management 8*(1): 15–24.

Anderson, Kristine J., Robert S. Freeman, Jean-Pierre V. M. Hérubel, Lawrence J. Mykytiuk, Judith M. Nixon, and Suzanne M. Ward. 2002. Buy, don't borrow: Bibliographers' analysis of academic library collection development through interlibrary loan requests. *Collection Management 27* (3/4): 1–10.

Blake, Julie C., and Susan P. Schleper. 2005. From data to decisions: Using surveys and statistics to make collection management decisions. *Library Collections, Acquisitions, and Technical Services 28*(4): 460–464.

Brug, Sandy, and Cristi MacWaters. 2004. Patron-driven purchasing from interlibrary loan requests. *Colorado Libraries 30*:36–38.

Byrd, Gary D., D. A. Thomas, and Katherine E. Hughes. 1982. Collection development using interlibrary loan borrowing and acquisitions statistics. *Bulletin of the Medical Library Association 70*(1): 1–9.

Carrigan, Dennis P. 1996. Data-guided collection development: A promise unfulfilled. *College & Research Libraries 57*(5): 429–437.

Chan, Gayle Rosemary Y. C. 2004. Purchase instead of borrow: An international perspective. *Journal of Interlibrary Loan Document Delivery and Information Supply 14*: 23–38.

Clendenning, Lynda Fuller. 2001. Purchase express for any user request: The University of Virginia Library offers delivery in seven days. *College & Research Libraries News 62*(1): 16–17.

Foss, Michelle. 2007. Books-on-demand pilot program: An innovative "patron-centric" approach to enhance the library collection. *Journal of Access Services 5*(1/2): 306–315.

Hulsey, Richard. 2003. Purchase on demand: A better customer service model. *Library Journal 128*(10): 77.

Kent, Allen. 1979. *Use of library materials : The University of Pittsburgh study*. New York: M. Dekker.

Knievel, Jennifer E., Heather Wicht, and Lynn Silipigni Connaway. 2006. Use of circulation statistics and interlibrary loan data in collection management. *College & Research Libraries 67*(1): 35.

Libraries, Association of Research. 2009. *ARL Statistics*, 2007–2008. http://www.arl.org/bm~doc/arlstat08.pdf.

Livingston, Camillo, and Antje Mays. 2004. Using interlibrary loan data as a selection tool: ILL trails provide collection clues. *Against the Grain 16*(2): 22–27.

Mortimore, Jeffrey M. 2006. Access-informed collection development and the academic library. *Collection Management 30*(3): 21–37.

New, Doris E, and Retha Zane Ott. 1974. Interlibrary loan analysis as a collection development tool. *Library Resources and Technical Services* 18(3): 275–283.

Perdue, Jennifer, and James A. Van Fleet. 1999. Borrow or buy? Cost-effective delivery of monographs. *Journal of Interlibrary Loan, Document Delivery & Information Supply* 9(4): 19–28.

Price, Jason, and John McDonald. *Beguiled by bananas? A retrospective study of usage and breadth of patron- vs. librarian-acquired ebook collections: Presentation on e-book acquisition at academic libraries given at XXIX Annual Charleston Conference: Issues in book and serial acquisition*, November 5, 2009. Available from http://ccdl.libraries.claremont.edu/cdm4/item_viewer.php?CISOROOT=/lea&CISOPTR=175&CISOBOX=1&REC=2.

Roberts, Michael, and Kenneth J. Cameron. 1984. A barometer of unmet demand. Interlibrary loans analysis and monographic acquisitions. *Library Acquisitions. Practice and Theory* 8(1): 31–42.

Ruppel, Margie. 2006. Tying collection development's loose ends with interlibrary loan. *Collection Building* 25(3): 72–77.

Trueswell, Richard L. 1969. Some behavioral patterns of library users: The 80/20 rule. *Wilson Library Bulletin* 43(5): 458–461.

Ward, Suzanne M. 2002. Books on demand: Just-in-time acquisitions. *Acquisitions Librarian* 27: 95–107.

Ward, Suzanne M., Tanner Wray, and Karl E. Debus-López. 2003. Collection development based on patron requests: Collaboration between interlibrary loan and acquisitions. *Library Collections, Acquisitions, and Technical Services* 27(2): 203–213.

Wender, Ruth W. 1969. Analysis of loans in the behavioral sciences. *Special Libraries* 60(8): 510–513.

Wood, David N., and Cathryn A. Bower. 1969. Survey of medical literature borrowed from the National Lending Library for Science and Technology. *Bulletin of the Medical Library Association* 57(1): 47.

Liberal Arts Books on Demand:
A Decade of Patron-Driven Collection
Development, Part 1

KRISTINE J. ANDERSON, ROBERT S. FREEMAN,
JEAN-PIERRE V. M. HÉRUBEL, LAWRENCE J. MYKYTIUK,
JUDITH M. NIXON, and SUZANNE M. WARD

Purdue University, West Lafayette, Indiana

The Purdue University Libraries was an early implementer of purchasing rather than borrowing books requested through interlibrary loan. This pioneering user-initiated acquisitions program, started in January 2000 and called Books on Demand, is managed by the interlibrary loan unit. Now that the program has reached its tenth year, the authors revisit their initial 2002 study to analyze books purchased in the six top subject areas across the whole decade. In their review of the liberal arts titles selected, subject librarians found that the books were appropriate additions and that these titles expanded the cross-disciplinary nature of the collection. The Books on Demand service offers a seamless method for all users, especially graduate students, to provide input into the collection building process.

INTRODUCTION

The Purdue University Libraries implemented the Books on Demand service in January 2000, buying—instead of borrowing—recently published English-language scholarly books submitted by users as interlibrary loan (ILL) requests (Ward 2002). In 2002, the authors analyzed requests from the departments that were major users of the service requesting about half the books purchased during the program's first two years and published the results (Anderson et al. 2002). At that time, the five bibliographers agreed that most of the purchased books were quality additions to the collection and that the service provided a path for graduate students' research needs to play a role in selection. A more surprising finding was the high number of books requested by scholars outside their subject fields. The librarians concluded that these cross-disciplinary requests were a significant enhancement to their collection development efforts.

This widely cited article (Anderson et al. 2002) was instrumental, at least in part, in convincing many other libraries to try this new approach of filling patrons' immediate needs while simultaneously building the collection with titles that would have a good chance of subsequent use. Similar programs were started at the libraries of Colorado State University (Brug and MacWaters 2004), Brigham Young University (Alder 2007), State University of New York-Buffalo (Bertuca et al. 2009), the University of Hong Kong (Chan 2004), and many other universities. The program was regarded as innovative and revolutionary in 2002; by 2009, many libraries of various sizes and types had incorporated some variation of the concept into their ILL operations or, convinced by the benefits of the concept behind user-initiated selection, pioneered other programs like patron selection of e-books.

In 2009, Purdue's Books on Demand program reached its tenth year. Nearly 10,000 books had been added to the collection based on ILL patron requests during the decade. The authors of the 2002 study were especially interested in digging deeper into the cross-disciplinary research trends that the first article uncovered. They decided to review the entire range of titles to date and to take a second look at these questions:

1. Who uses the service? Are the primary users students or faculty? What departmental affiliates make the heaviest use of the service?
2. Do the affiliates of the top user departments order books that are *in scope* for the collection?
3. Does a comparison of the departmental affiliations and the call numbers indicate an increase in the cross-disciplinary research seen in the two-year study? What subjects are the most in demand?
4. Are the books purchased for Books on Demand *appropriate* for the collection? Are the books from university or scholarly publishers?
5. Why are far fewer books in science/technology being added than in the liberal arts?
6. Once they are on the shelves, are the books purchased for Books on Demand more heavily used than books acquired through regular collection development activities?

This article answers the first four of these questions; the other two will be addressed in separate articles in this issue. The purpose of this ten-year review is to determine whether the program is still as effective now as it was judged to be in its early stages and to see whether a decade of data reveals any important or interesting trends that had not been evident with only two years of data in 2002.

Books on Demand Criteria

In 2002, ILL book requests would be purchased if they met these criteria:

- In English
- Nonfiction
- Scholarly
- Published within the past five years
- Maximum cost of $150
- Shipment within one week from an online bookseller

By 2009, the criteria had changed only slightly; the publication range was changed to the past three years and DVDs that meet the criteria were also purchased. The English language requirement was relaxed so that on rare occasions some very recent non-English titles could be purchased from amazon.de or amazon.fr if there was no other way to obtain a copy quickly through normal ILL channels. Determining when a book meets the criteria is the responsibility of an ILL borrowing assistant. From the outset, there has been no librarian review of titles before purchase. This decision was an important factor in the initial proposal; the program did not require librarians' time nor was it slowed down by waiting for librarian approval of purchases. The same employee has made almost all the purchase decisions for the program's entire duration. This staff mediation is an important element in the selection process as it provides a quick filter to eliminate titles such as textbooks and popular or hobby-related books. While the definition of "scholarly" may differ from one person to another, the same person has applied the same definition for ten years. She has taken into consideration such factors as whether it would sometimes be appropriate to buy slightly less scholarly titles to meet undergraduate requestors' needs. She also has decided which campus library eventually receives each cataloged book following the ILL patron's initial use.

METHODOLOGY

To compile ten years of the data for this research, the Books on Demand records were downloaded from the ILL databases and imported into a Microsoft Access database. During the past ten years, Purdue's ILL unit has used two management systems, Clio and then ILLiad[1]; the first step required integrating records from both ILL systems into one list. Besides compiling bibliographic information, it was important to capture users' status and departmental affiliations and the dates the requests were filled. This information was then enhanced by matching it with data from Purdue's integrated library system (ILS), the Voyager Library System, to add call numbers and first subject headings. Of all the steps in the process, the match of ILL data and Voyager data was the most problematic as most of the titles in the ILL systems varied slightly from the titles in Voyager. If even a slight variation existed, the records did not merge. The final solution was to match on the first few letters of the titles, an ingenious and successful solution, but one that required considerable manual review. Also, a few books had been lost by patrons and therefore did not have call numbers. Since they represent books requested as part of the Books on Demand program, they remained in the database but were not used in the call number analysis.

Analysis of Users: Who Uses the Service?

GRADUATE LIBERAL ARTS STUDENTS ARE THE PRIMARY USERS

A total of 9,572 books were purchased through Books on Demand during the ten years from 2000 to 2009.[2] The original study reviewed the books requested by users in the six subject departments that had most heavily benefited from the service: English, Foreign Languages & Literatures, History, Management, Philosophy, and Political Science. It reviewed all the titles in the call number ranges that corresponded with these six departments. This current study analyzes the books requested by patrons with the same six departmental affiliations between 2000 and 2009, thus including the ones purchased during the time period of the first study. During the original study, patrons from these six departments requested 45% of the books purchased. The percentage increased from 45% to 49% of the total purchases between 2000 and 2009. The authors had anticipated that as the service became better known, patrons from other departments would make heavier use of it, but this has not been the case (Table 1).

These six departments are all in the liberal arts, a somewhat surprising result since Purdue University has a strong science/technology focus, with 58% of its students enrolled in a science/technology field such as agriculture, engineering, or one of the pure sciences; only 37% of the students are in the liberal arts (Office 2010). Yet users in these six liberal arts fields requested 6,212 books, or 65% of the total. And even more surprising is that 82% of the Books on Demand titles fall into liberal arts call number ranges; only 13% fall into the science/technology ranges. One explanation might be that the science/technology users are more journal-focused than book-focused; the fact that they are frequently seeking solutions to specific problems makes them less "big picture"–focused and therefore less interested in reading books.

TABLE 1 Number of Books Requested by Six Heavy-Use Departments; Comparing the First 2 Years With the Ten-Year Study

Department	Number Requested by Departmental Affiliates 2000–2002	Number Requested by Departmental Affiliates 2000–2009
English	231	1748
Foreign Languages & Literatures	138	606
History	88	1182
Management	67	239
Philosophy	58	399
Political Science	70	474
Total	652	4648

Another possible explanation is that books in the science and technology areas are higher-priced, but with the Books on Demand maximum price set at $150 this does not seem likely. One other idea brought forward, although difficult to prove, is that users of the science and technology book collections find them more adequate than do users of the liberal arts collection. This imbalance between the size of the science/technology user base and number of Books on Demand science/technology titles prompted Marianne Stowell Bracke, a Purdue science librarian, to investigate this trend more fully. Her study is the subject of a separate article in this issue.

Table 2 shows that graduate students constitute the major user category from these six departments. Undergraduates are a very small percentage of the users. This result was true of the two-year study, and the ten-year data show little difference. These statistics are consistent with Purdue's overall interlibrary loan service, with approximately 70% of the use from graduate and undergraduate students. Graduate students affiliated with the English department requested a greater percentage than the average, and Foreign Languages & Literatures graduate students less than the average. So the investigation of user status reveals consistency with ILL use.

TABLE 2 Percentage of Books Requested, by Departmental Affiliation and Patron Category

Department	Faculty or Staff Percentage	Graduate Student Percentage	Undergraduate Student Percentage
English	20%	76%	3%
Foreign Languages & Literatures	50%	44%	3%
History	35%	57%	7%
Management	25%	66%	9%
Philosophy	31%	68%	1%
Political Science	34%	58%	4%

TABLE 3 Percentage of the Books on Demand Titles *Requested by Departmental Affiliates* and Evaluated as In Scope by Bibliographers

Department	No. Ordered by Department Affiliates 2000–2009	No. Librarian Found as In Department Scope 2009	Percentage In Department Scope 2009
English	1748	1377	79%
Foreign Languages & Literatures	606	529	87%
History	1182	1039	88%
Management	239	213	89%
Philosophy	399	371	93%
Political Science	474	417	88%
Total	4648	3946	85%

Bibliographers' Analysis

To dig deeper into the data, the same bibliographers who conducted the 2002 study analyzed the titles in their subject areas using two approaches:

- Books requested by their departments' affiliates
- Books with call numbers corresponding to the departments' subject focus

Are books requested by these six departmental affiliates in scope for the collection?

Yes, 79% to 93% are. Each bibliographer determined whether the books requested by his or her departmental affiliates were *in scope* for that subject area. Books were considered out of scope if the librarian would not have used department allocations to purchase the book. The call number assigned the book had no bearing on this review. Rather, the librarian looked at the title, publisher, and subject heading to identify out-of-scope titles. Overall, 79% to 93% of the titles were identified as in scope. Table 3 summarizes these results.

Does a comparison of the departmental affiliations and the call numbers indicate an increase in the cross-disciplinary research seen in the two-year study?

Yes, cross disciplinary research has increased. An analysis of the *call numbers of the books requested by departmental affiliates* in Table 4 indicates that although most books requested were judged by the librarian as in scope or in disciplinary alignment, only about half or fewer fell within the call number ranges associated with the subject. Table 4 lists the primary call number ranges for each subject.[3] This observation prompted the bibliographers to take a closer look at the titles, subject headings, and publishers of these books to see whether this phenomenon could be explained by requests for personal development or recreational reading. Based on this title-by-title examination, all the bibliographers saw subject interests in related or tangential

TABLE 4 Number of Books Ordered by Departmental Affiliates Compared to the Number of Books Ordered That Are within Subject Call Number Ranges

Department	No. Ordered by Department	Call No.	No. of Books Ordered by Department within Call No.	Percentage of Books Requested by Department in Call No.
English	1748	410s +800–829 +PE/PN/PZ	690	39%
Foreign Languages & Literatures	606	400's + 830–899 +P's	114	19%
History	1182	900's = D*/E*/F*	430	36%
Management	239	330+332+338+ 650's +HB:HJ	135	56%
Philosophy	399	100:149+160:199 +B:BD +BH:BJ	224	56%
Political Science	474	320's +J's	145	31%
Total	4648		1738	37%

fields that indicated strong cross-disciplinary interests. These following examples help to illustrate the types of apparently out-of-scope subjects that actually indicate that researchers are delving into research in related fields: a philosophy patron interested in issues in women's studies; a management patron interested in database structure; a political scientist interested in environmental studies; an English scholar requesting books on film studies. For most of these out-of-call number range books, the scholarly need for the title was obvious, either because it provided background material or was part of an interdisciplinary research area such as women's studies or American studies. Although it was impossible to show by quantifiable data that the cause was cross-disciplinary research, the bibliographers agreed that this was the most logical explanation. Only occasionally did an idiosyncratic interest surface, such as books on personal medical concerns or hobby-related titles.

Another way to see cross-disciplinary research trends is to look at the total number of books within a call number range and see how many were requested by departmental affiliates. Table 5 indicates a wide variation in these six subject areas, with English and philosophy affiliates requesting a greater percentage of the books bought in their field. The most noticeable fact in Table 5 is that the management affiliates requested only 18% of the books in the management call numbers. More than 80% of the management books were requested by non-management faculty and students. This heavy use of the management literature caused a spike in the number of books acquired on this subject, for a total of 770 books, or 8% of the all the Books on Demand titles. This is the figure even when defining the Dewey call number range narrowly as 330, 332, or 338 or any of the 650s. This result prompted a more careful look at these books and the home departments of these requestors. There are several departments on campus that have a strong management component, so the librarian expected heavy use from non-management patrons from the departments such as Consumer Science & Retailing, Hospitality & Tourism Management, and Organizational Leadership & Supervision. However, the top departments were actually Communication, Agricultural Economics, Consumer Science & Retailing, Library Science, English, Industrial Engineering, Political Science, and History. The only department in this list that the bibliographer had anticipated was Consumer Science & Retailing. These results demonstrate strong cross-disciplinary use of the management literature by faculty and students in the liberal arts and in the engineering/technology colleges. One of the high-use groups is librarians, a group that does not include any students since Purdue does not have a Library Science program. Just like the Purdue librarians, many Purdue users are interested in management topics. Areas of high interest are advertising and brand names, business intelligence and logistics, presentations and meetings, consumers and customers, electronic commerce and games, economic topics, employment and leadership, organizational change, finance, industry, and marketing.

TABLE 5 Comparison of the Number of Books Requested by Each Discipline's Affiliates with Number of Books in the Discipline's Subject Class Ranges

Department	No. Requested by Department Affiliates	Call No.	Total No. of Books on Demand in Call No.	Books Requested by Department in Call No.	Percentage Requested by Department in Call No.
English	1748	410s +800–829 +PE/PN/PZ	1111	690	62%
Foreign Languages & Literatures	606	400's + 830–899 +P's	386	114	30%
History	1182	900's = D*/E*/F*	993	430	43%
Management	239	330+332+338+ 650's +HB:HJ	770	135	18%
Philosophy	399	100:149+160:199 +B:BD +BH:BJ	449	224	50%
Political Science	474	320's +J's	396	145	37%
Total	4648		4105	1738	42%

A similar trend is evident in books requested in the sociology and religion call numbers. Only 12% of the books in sociology call numbers were requested by faculty or students from the Sociology or Anthropology departments. And, likewise, only 12% of the books in religion were requested by philosophy users.[4] Both these areas, like management, are heavily used by the nonprimary users. This presents a challenge for normal collection development procedures. The librarians building the management, sociology, and religion collections need to be aware that those areas are of high interest to many on campus. This finding also indicates that the Books on Demand project can be of significant importance in building the collection in these areas.

Are the books purchased for Books on Demand appropriate for the collection? Are the books from university or scholarly publishers?

Yes, the books fit well into Purdue's collection development scope.   In the analysis by call number, the librarians found that very few books were added to the collection that were too popular or in other ways *inappropriate* for a university library collection (Table 6). Even in the management area, where a few "get rich quick" books and a few popular-style management books slipped into the collection, only about 5% of the books were deemed inappropriate. This is an extremely small percentage of the total number of books acquired.

Another way to determine whether users are requesting appropriate books is to look at the publishers by categories (university, academic, or trade/popular presses) of the books requested. Table 7 indicates that approximately half of the books were published by university presses and another 37% by academic presses, so nearly 90% of the requested books were from scholarly presses. Only 12% were from trade or popular presses. Based on the publisher analysis, users are asking for books that are appropriate for the collection. The publishers most requested by these six departments were Cambridge University Press, Routledge, and Oxford University Press. Table 8 lists the top 25 publishers and the number of books purchased from them; 18 of the 25 are university presses. Taken together, these 25 publishers supplied more than 40% of the requested titles.

USER RESPONSE TO THE BOOKS ON DEMAND PROGRAM

As each book was received and processed, ILL staff slipped a paper flag between the pages. The flag briefly explained that the book had been purchased in response to the ILL request and that the book would be added to the library collection after the initial two-week loan. The flag asked patrons to answer two questions: (1) had the book arrived on time to meet their need; and (2) in the users' opinion, was the book very useful, moderately useful, or marginally useful as an addition to the collection?

TABLE 6 Appropriateness of Books within Call Number Ranges for Purdue's Collection

Department	Call No.	Total No. of Books on Demand in Call No.	No. Inappropriate for the Collection	No. Appropriate	Percentage Appropriate
English	410s +800–829 +PE/PN/PZ	1111	1	1110	99.9%
Foreign Languages & Literatures	400's + 830–899 +P's	386	3	383	99.2%
History	900's = D*/E*/F*	993	3	990	99.7%
Management	330+332+338+ 650's +HB:HJ	770	39	731	94.9%
Philosophy	100:149+160:199 +B:BD +BH:BJ	449	0	449	100.0%
Political Science	320's +J's	396	0	396	100.0%
Total		4105	46	4059	98.9%

TABLE 7 What Percentage of Titles Were from University Presses? Academic/Scholarly Presses? Trade Presses or Popular Presses?

Department	No. Ordered by Departmental Affiliates	University	Percentage University	Academic	Percentage Academic	Popular/Trade	Percentage Popular/Trade
English	1748	815	47%	711	41%	222	13%
Foreign Languages & Literatures	606	271	45%	223	37%	111	18%
History	1182	674	57%	290	25%	218	18%
Management	239	60	25%	140	59%	34	14%
Philosophy	399	209	52%	155	39%	35	9%
Political Science	474	230	49%	189	40%	55	12%
Total	4648	2253	48%	1647	37%	541	12%

TABLE 8 Top Publishers for Books Requested by the Six Major Departments

Publisher	Type	Number
Cambridge University Press	University	255
Routledge	Academic	242
Oxford University Press	University	228
Palgrave	Academic	106
Princeton University Press	University	78
Duke University Press	University	75
Blackwell	Academic	72
University of California Press	University	71
University of Chicago Press	University	67
Rowman & Littlefield	Academic	64
State University of New York Press	University	61
MIT Press	University	49
University of Minnesota Press	University	48
Yale University Press	University	48
Ashgate	Academic	46
Cornell University Press	University	44
Harvard University Press	University	41
Rodopi	Academic	41
Johns Hopkins University Press	University	40
Sage	Academic	39
Stanford University Press	University	38
Clarendon Press; Oxford University	University	37
University of Pennsylvania Press	University	37
University of North Carolina Press	University	36
University of Illinois Press	University	35

Table 9 summarizes patron responses to these two questions in the spring 2002 and spring 2008 semesters. Not all books were returned with the paper flags filled out. Table 9 shows results only from those flags with completed questionnaires, but responding patrons reported overwhelmingly that the books arrived quickly. They also agreed that most of the books were very useful additions to the collection (90% in spring 2008). Some patrons also wrote comments on the flags, many of them remarking about the books' speedy arrival. Several said that they would check the books out again after they were cataloged to enjoy the longer loan period and unlimited renewals for cataloged books. Others pointed out that a particular book filled a gap in the collection. Occasionally, users noted that a book had not turned out

TABLE 9 Patrons' Satisfaction

	Spring 2002			Spring 2008		
Timely arrival	Yes	No		Yes	No	
	257	5		307	2	
Book's usefulness	Very	Moderately	Marginally	Very	Moderately	Marginally
	265	28	6	277	27	5

to be as helpful as anticipated for their immediate needs but that it was still a good addition to the collection. The Appendix lists selected patron comments about the Books on Demand program.

CONCLUSIONS

This study looked at four questions about books ordered based on ILL requests: Who uses the service? Do the users from the heaviest user departments request books that are in scope for their respective subjects? Has there been an increase in the cross-disciplinary research seen in the first study in 2002? And are the books appropriate for the collection?

Patrons from the same six liberal arts departments—English, Foreign Languages & Literatures, History, Management, Philosophy, and Political Science—who were the heavy users in 2002 continued to be heavy users. As a group, they requested nearly 50% of the Books on Demand titles. Graduate students are the predominant users; they requested more than 60% of the titles. The analysis of the titles by these six departmental affiliates shows that 79% to 93% of the books are in scope and would have been purchased with departmental funds by the librarian. However, every librarian saw high demand for in books in divergent or tangential fields. This confirmed the strong cross-disciplinary research trends seen in the first study. The call number analysis revealed an even stronger confirmation of the cross-disciplinary research. A range of 40% to 80% of the books within subject call numbers were requested by users outside the subject field. Although this trend is evident in all the liberal arts areas, management, religion, and sociology show the heaviest use from patrons across campus. Despite that users across campus request a large number of ILL books that are outside their subject fields, the librarians found that 98% of the books were appropriate to a research library. Reviewing books' publishers indicated the same appropriateness. Users found the service timely and judged that the vast majority of the books that were purchased based on their ILL requests were appropriate for the collection.

Past collection development policies and procedures have given librarians and faculty members the major responsibility of shaping and developing the collection. Bibliographers in the liberal arts, especially in the humanities areas at Purdue, have relied heavily on faculty recommendations when selecting books. Graduate students, who are the major users of the book collection and the most avant garde researchers, have had little opportunity to contribute in the selection of books. This study shows that users do request books through the ILL service that are very appropriate for the collection. Regardless of which way the purchases were analyzed—by requester status, requester departmental affiliation, by call number, or by publisher type—almost all the books complement the library's collection. Since the major users are graduate students, this service provides a very convenient path for their input. In some ways, the results of this study call into question the traditional practice of relying heavily on faculty advice, which may ignore the most current topics of research that graduate students are embracing. It suggests that subject selectors should find or add to the ways of soliciting suggestions from graduate students.

However, the bibliographers involved in this study also argue against the idea that collection development be left *completely* up to users. They think it imperative that Books on Demand should not be the only approach; it is simply an advantageous tool, one of several avenues for developing collections. Relying on users alone could lead to a misshapen collection; as in the past when departmental faculty members had the responsibility for developing the collection and one or two faculty members spent all the departmental allocation on their narrow research area. Librarians need to accept the responsibility of developing the collection and, as subject experts with the knowledge provided by reference experience, provide the critical balance to the collection, ensuring that both current research and pedagogical needs are represented. Making new purchases from the ILL requests has proven to be a very effective method for Purdue to involve users at all levels in the development of the collection. The beauty of Books on Demand is that it addresses actual research needs, especially those of graduate students, without imposing any particular ideology of collection development or placing demands on the users' time. In conclusion, the liberal arts librarians support increasing the percentage of funding allocated to Books on Demand, even doubling the funds.

ACKNOWLEDGEMENTS

The authors gratefully acknowledge Amy Winks for extracting the raw data from the Clio and ILLiad databases and E. Stewart Saunders for compiling the master Microsoft Access database.

NOTES

1. Clio from Clio Software (www.cliosoftware.com) and ILLiad from OCLC/Atlas Systems (www.oclc.org/illiad).

2. The data for the study were gathered in mid 2009, so although this article often mentions a decade, the actual data examined cover nine years and seven months.

3. In 2009, the Purdue Libraries changed from Dewey Decimal classification to Library of Congress classification, so there were 98 books with Library of Congress call numbers. These were added to the subject call number lists for each bibliographer and are included in the statistics.

4. Religious Studies was part of the Philosophy department during most of the time covered by this study.

REFERENCES

Alder, Nancy Lichten. 2007. Direct purchase as a function of interlibrary loan: Buying books versus borrowing. *Journal of Interlibrary Loan, Document Delivery & Electronic Reserves 18*(1): 9–15.

Anderson, Kristine J., Robert S. Freeman, Jean-Pierre V. M. Hérubel, Lawrence J. Mykytiuk, Judith M. Nixon, and Suzanne M. Ward. 2002. Buy, don't borrow: Bibliographers' analysis of academic library collection development through interlibrary loan requests. *Collection Management 27*(3/4): 1–10.

Bertuca, Cynthia, Carol Lelonek, Rena Tuohy, Jill Ortner, Anne Bouvier, Sarah Dithomas, Suzanne Hayes, and Sarah Morehouse. 2009. Two ILLiad clients, one desktop, purchase on demand: Sharing a university's collection, staff, and expertise. *Journal of Access Services 6*(4): 497–512.

Brug, Sandy, and Cristi MacWaters. 2004. Patron-driven purchasing from interlibrary loan requests. *Colorado Libraries 30*: 36–38.

Chan, Gayle Rosemary Y. C. 2004. Purchase instead of borrow: An international perspective. *Journal of Interlibrary Loan Document Delivery and Information Supply 14*: 23–38.

Office of Institutional Research, Purdue University. 2010. *Purdue University data digest: Enrollment by college/school and by student level—West Lafayette Campus (for fall semester in academic years 2000–01 through 2009–2010)*. Available from http://www.purdue.edu/datadigest/pages/students/stu_sch_level.htm (Accessed May 25, 2010).

Ward, Suzanne M. 2002. Books on demand: Just-in-time acquisitions. *The Acquisitions Librarian 27*: 95–107.

APPENDIX: SELECTED PATRON COMMENTS

I was truly impressed by this new approach to interlibrary loan: it will benefit many other students & researchers. Thank you. (2008)

This book will be used a lot by students in the English and American Studies programs. (2002)

This is a tremendous service! Thank you for the very speedy response to my request! (2002)

This book is not very useful to me, but [it] may well be useful to colleagues in other disciplines. (2008)

I'll be checking it out soon. (2002)

Good idea! I've asked for interlibrary loans before, and this time it was quicker. (2002)

I think it is a very good idea to make acquisitions in this way. This book will be in demand. (2002)

On behalf of the Early Americanists in the English Dept, THANK YOU! (2008)

The book came so much faster than I ever expected! (2002)

This is a very important book and would be a distinguished addition to the current library collection. (2002).

There are few publications that applied oral tradition to the transmission of synoptic tradition. This is a very valuable book. (2008)

I had this book within two days of my request. Very impressive! (2002)

Wow! Do it again! (2002)

Science and Technology Books on Demand: A Decade of Patron-Driven Collection Development, Part 2

MARIANNE STOWELL BRACKE

Purdue University, West Lafayette, Indiana

The Purdue University Libraries have been participating in a patron-driven collection development project for 10 years. This analysis focuses on the books purchased in the science and technology areas. The author found that the books were appropriate and in many cases identified emerging or interdisciplinary topics that might have been missed by librarians. In addition, data proved to be a rich source of information for collecting, such as identifying publishers or emerging areas that warranted further attention from selectors. Although not replacing librarians as the major collection developers, patron-driven selection is one successful way to augment collection development.

INTRODUCTION

Academic librarians face many challenges in building a monograph collection for their institutions. They must build a collection that satisfies both the immediate needs of a diverse group of users while creating a coherent research collection for the future. Some needs are immediate, some are transient, and others will only be realized in the future. There never seems to be enough money to purchase everything that a librarian would wish to add to a collection, yet some books sit on the shelf unused, still awaiting that first checkout.

Librarians with responsibilities in science and technology encounter additional challenges. The collection budget must be balanced meaningfully between books and journals, yet the majority of the budget often goes to support journal subscriptions and their steady inflationary increases. The limited budget means that books must be carefully selected. Adding a patron-driven selection component to overall collection development strategies can be one way to capitalize on purchases that meet current demands. The data collected can also help inform selectors of unmet needs and emerging areas of research.

BACKGROUND

In January 2000, the Purdue Libraries began to pilot a Books on Demand project through the interlibrary loan (ILL) department. The program explored patron-driven selection as a way to augment current collection development practices. The goal was to provide needed materials in a more timely fashion as well as identify disciplinary areas that may be emerging or are not fully addressed by standard collection methods. The criteria for purchasing these books were that they be scholarly nonfiction works, published within the past five years, costing no more than $150, and available for shipment within one week from an online bookseller. Determining whether a book was "scholarly" was an imperfect process that ultimately depended on the best judgment of the ILL staff. The ILL staff reviewed incoming requests against the above criteria to determine whether they belonged in this program or should be ordered through conventional ILL methods. The staff also decided which campus library should house the books purchased, based upon the patron's departmental affiliation and the disciplinary nature of the book. Patrons were not aware of the program and assumed they were ordering as usual through ILL.

Early in the process, librarians performed an in-depth analysis for the top six disciplines. These six comprised almost half of the requests, and the librarians determined that these books were appropriate to add to the collection in 80% to 99% of the cases, varying by discipline (Anderson et al. 2002). Not surprisingly, these disciplines were all in the humanities and social sciences,[1] where scholars, it is typically assumed, use more books than they do in science and technology. The science and technology titles were not studied in the initial project because they made up such a small percentage. Ten years later, close to 10,000 titles have been purchased. Of these, roughly 15%, or 1,557 titles, fall in the areas of science and technology. This seems like a curiously small percentage given Purdue University's heavy emphasis on science, technology, engineering, and medicine, or the STEM disciplines. Due to the relatively low number of titles, the author was able to assess books in all areas of science and technology, unlike in the initial and subsequent studies of the humanities and social sciences, where different selectors assessed each discipline.

This study set out to determine whether the Books on Demand program has been successful as a means of supplementing traditional collection development methods for science and technology disciplines. It analyzes this issue by addressing three questions:

1. Are the titles acquired through the program ones that are in scope for a science and technology research collection?
2. Has the program helped to develop a more appropriate collection for science and technology areas by filling gaps in collections, especially in interdisciplinary areas, and by identifying new areas of emphasis and publishers for selectors?
3. Has the program led to the acquisition of scholarly titles that are relevant to the campus community broadly, beyond the obvious needs of STEM disciplines?

METHODOLOGY

This analysis covers books in the areas of science and technology as defined through several means. Due to a number of factors, including Purdue's continued use of the Dewey Decimal system until 2009 and Purdue's decentralized library system that includes numerous discipline-specific campus libraries and an undergraduate library, it was complicated to establish a set of books that could easily be defined as science and technology. The final set includes books that fell into the Dewey 500 to 699[2] call number range (excluding the 650 to 659 range for management) and reside in any library location. However, the study also reviewed books that fell outside of that call number range but were placed through this program into the following science libraries: Chemistry, Earth & Atmospheric Sciences, Engineering, Life Sciences, Mathematical Sciences, Pharmacy, Nursing & Health Sciences, Physics, and Veterinary Medicine. These books included items covering software or computer programming and management that may be needed in the sciences but, because of the multifaceted focus, were assigned a call number outside of the science-specific ranges. The call number–defined data set included 1,201 titles, while books that fell outside of that call number range but were sent to one of the science libraries added an additional 356 titles. So 23% of the total data set of 1,557 titles had non-science call numbers. The total data set was assessed for books that would have been appropriate to add to the collection, while the call number–only subset was used to compare circulation data. This distinction was due to the inability to create a circulation data set that matched the entire data set.

The author used an Access file created from the ILL data combined with circulation data. The file included the following fields automatically generated from either the ILL system or the circulation system: book title, author, year published, library sent to, department of requestor (when available), complete call number, three-digit call number, main subject headings, total circulations, total circulations (by faculty, by graduate students, and by undergraduates), total renewals, browses, received date, and days since received. Additionally, the author created fields for type of publisher (university press, scholarly/professional, and popular/trade) and whether a book was appropriate for the collection. The author used professional judgment in assigning values in these last two fields.

The publisher type was determined by several factors. Presses affiliated with universities or colleges were assigned accordingly (e.g., Oxford University Press, Duke University Press). The rest were assigned to scholarly/professional (e.g., CABI, CRC Press, American Psychiatric Press) or popular/trade (e.g., Penguin, St. Martin's Press) by overall catalog of titles sold. Publisher type was one factor in determining whether a title would be appropriate to add to the collection. University press titles and scholarly/professional were generally deemed appropriate (with the exception of two

TABLE 1 Top Publishers for Science and Technology Books

Publisher	Type of Publisher	No. of Books
Springer	Scholarly/professional	148
Wiley	Scholarly/professional	112
Cambridge University Press	University	75
Elsevier	Scholarly/professional	67
Pearson Education	Scholarly/professional	65
Oxford University Press	University	63
Taylor & Francis	Scholarly/professional	42
CRC Press	Scholarly/professional	41
Kluwer	Scholarly/professional	40
Guilford Press	Scholarly/professional	33
McGraw-Hill	Scholarly/professional	24
Sage Publications	Scholarly/professional	22
Princeton University Press	University	19
Lawrence Erlbaum	Scholarly/professional	18
MIT Press	University	16
World Scientific	Scholarly/professional	16
Artech House	Scholarly/professional	11
A K Peters	Scholarly/professional	10
Island Press	Scholarly/professional	10
O'Reilly	Scholarly/professional	10
University of Chicago Press	University	10
Yale University Press	University	10

titles). Table 1 lists the top publishers for which the science and technology libraries received 10 or more books from the Books on Demand project.

Other books were reviewed for appropriateness by reading book reviews, checking main subject headings, and determining whether they filled an academic need of the collection. For instance, a non–science major undergraduate may need a more general work on a scientific topic than would a faculty member in the sciences.

ANALYSIS

In Scope for a Science and Technology Research Collection

Overwhelmingly, the Books on Demand titles were books that belonged in the research collection. Of the total science and technology data set, 64 titles, or only 4%, were judged by the author not to be appropriate. These titles were deemed too popular or general to have actually met the "scholarly" criteria of the program. They included books aimed at a juvenile audience or were self-help books on relationships, health, disease, and diets. The titles that were deemed in scope were ones librarians would have added anyway to fill needs of students, staff, or faculty on campus in the course of routine collection development.

That 96% of the titles were deemed in scope illustrates the importance of collecting holistically, in other words, in a manner that was conscious of the needs of all levels and disciplines represented on campus. Librarians with a liaison role with a particular department and a responsibility for collection funds in that area may make it a priority to select titles to serve those faculty and students. However, on a large campus with more than 40,000 undergraduates, graduates, researchers, instructors, staff, and faculty, the information needs are quite diverse. Analyzing the books selected in a program such as this can give a selector insight into those varying needs. For instance, many of the books were interdisciplinary between sciences, such as biology and mathematics, but many were interdisciplinary between sciences and the social sciences, such as the history of food or the philosophy of medical research. Additionally, books were selected and deemed in scope that approached topics from the most basic (e.g., a cell biology textbook) to the most advanced (e.g., cutting-edge stem cell research), reflecting the many different knowledge levels of library users.

Circulation figures for the books are listed in Table 2. Of the 1,557 titles, only 269, or 17%, have not circulated beyond the initial ILL request. This is higher circulation than we normally see, and it indicates the appropriateness of the Books on Demand titles. Additionally, delving further into those 269 titles, 88, or one-third, have been owned for two years or less. This set of books may certainly circulate more times. Many of these 1,557 books had

TABLE 2 Circulation Totals for Science and Technology Books, 2000–2009

No. of Total Checkouts	No. of Books in This Category	Percentage of Total Books Purchased for Program
40–79	10	<1%
20–39	48	3%
10–19	167	11%
5–9	344	22%
4	188	12%
3	242	16%
2	289	19%
1	269	17%

high circulation numbers; more than 36% of the titles had circulated five or more times in the time period.

Richer Areas of Collection for Interdisciplinary and Emerging Areas in STEM Disciplines

This program helped to develop underrepresented, interdisciplinary, and emerging areas of the science and technology collections. The data subset of titles that fell outside of the call number ranges but were placed in one of the science libraries is especially useful in this way. For instance, this data set showed three areas of importance. First, there were a large number of computer and networking books. These are books that may have a short shelf life, as the technology they describe changes or becomes obsolete, yet they fulfill an immediate need for current information and often have high circulation rates. Because the need for these types of books is brief yet timely, users may be the best judge of which titles to select. Second, there were also a substantial number of books on environmental issues, an area that crosses social, life, and applied scientific disciplines yet often falls outside of the 500 to 699 call number range. In this instance, one publisher, Island Press, appeared 10 times and signaled that this may be a publisher that was falling through the cracks between disciplines. Ten is a small number when compared to the number of books acquired from large publishers such as Wiley, but it does illustrate the need for special attention to be paid to a niche publisher. Finally, there were a noteworthy number of titles on Geographic Information Systems, an emerging area of study at the university.

Access to Titles That Serve the Broader Campus

This project also illustrated the use of science and technology books across campus. Collection librarians often focus primarily on serving the needs of

TABLE 3 Number and Percentage of Requests by User Status

User Status	No. of Requests	Percentage of Requests
Graduate students	946	61%
Faculty	284	18%
Staff	171	11%
Undergraduate students	141	9%
Visiting scholars	14	<1%
Other	1	<1%

the departments for which they are liaisons. However, this leaves out numerous users that may be affiliated with campus but not with a disciplinary department. Requests came not only from departments (e.g., Biology, English, Chemistry), but from more than 100 different interdisciplinary and administrative units (e.g., Purdue University Interdisciplinary Life Science Ph.D. Program, the Office of the Vice President for Research, Counseling and Psychological Services) and research centers (e.g., Discovery Learning Center) across campus.

Use was also noted across user status (Table 3).

FURTHER RESEARCH

This project has some limitations for study. For instance, there is no list of books that were considered by ILL for inclusion in this project but were rejected for any number of reasons: ILL staff considered the book not scholarly, price exceeded $150, or it was not immediately available for purchase. This would be a useful list for subject selectors to have for review. They might recognize areas of study, particularly emerging or interdisciplinary areas, that might be discounted by ILL staff as not scholarly or not recognized as an emerging pattern of need.

Additionally, this is just a preliminary review of this data set. There are many opportunities for further in-depth research. One question that remains unanswered given the limitations of the current data and of ILL procedures is why the percentage of books purchased is so low in the science and technology disciplines (as defined by call number or by campus library). For example, 33% of all monographs purchased by Purdue in 2007 and 2008 were designated for one of the science libraries. In contrast, only about 15% of the Books on Demand titles were in science and technology disciplines (as defined in this study). The price cap of $150 does not seem to be an obvious barrier, as illustrated in Table 4. When averaging the cost of books purchased through approval plans and firm orders across two years by science libraries, in only one instance, the Chemistry Library in 2007, did the average price exceed the limit. In fact, average costs were below or near $100.

TABLE 4 Average Cost of Books Purchased by Campus Library, 2007–2008

Library Location	2007 Average Cost/Book	2008 Average Cost/Book
Chemistry	$155	$115
Earth & Atmospheric Sciences	$76	$81
Engineering	$107	$102
Life Sciences	$96	$101
Mathematical Sciences	$74	$74
Pharmacy, Nursing & Health Sciences	$93	$99
Physics	$83	$85
Veterinary Medicine	$98	$108

There may be other explanations, such as procedural issues within the libraries, information-seeking behaviors among user populations, differences in the relationship between researchers and the libraries, or a combination of these and other factors. At this point, limitations in the available data make it difficult if not impossible to determine why there is such a large difference in percentage between books purchased on-demand and all other monographs received. Additional data gathering may shed more light on this issue, which could have important implications for librarianship in the STEM disciplines.

CONCLUSION

A patron-driven selection model is a successful way to augment current collection strategies, especially in science and technology disciplines. It may catch emerging or interdisciplinary trends of study. Users who are pushing the boundaries of research are more familiar with the changes in their field. They are better able to express a need that may take longer for librarians to recognize. The model also takes advantage of real user need to read titles of immediate, but perhaps time-limited, impact. Computer or software books are such an example: many books are published in such topics, but no library can afford to buy all of them. User selection is one way to help identify which ones are truly needed. However, it is important to note that user selection cannot replace librarian selection entirely. Librarians are still needed to make the collection more coherent and useful as a long-term research collection. User selection can help fill niches, but librarians are responsible for making sure the collection is well-rounded.

ACKNOWLEDGEMENTS

The author gratefully acknowledges Amy Winks for extracting the raw data from the Clio and ILLiad databases and E. Stewart Saunders for compiling the master Microsoft Access database.

NOTES

1. History, English, Foreign Languages & Literatures, Political Science, Management, and Philosophy.

2. The 500 call number range is for Natural Sciences and Mathematics, while the 600 range includes Technology and the Applied Sciences.

REFERENCE

Anderson, Kristine J., Robert S. Freeman, Jean-Pierre V. M. Hérubel, Lawrence J. Mykytiuk, Judith M. Nixon, and Suzanne M. Ward. 2002. Buy, don't borrow: Bibliographers' analysis of academic library collection development through interlibrary loan requests. *Collection Management* 27(3/4): 1–10.

A Study of Circulation Statistics of Books on Demand: A Decade of Patron-Driven Collection Development, Part 3

JUDITH M. NIXON and E. STEWART SAUNDERS

Purdue University, West Lafayette, Indiana

The Purdue University Libraries was an early implementer of purchasing books requested through interlibrary loan rather than borrowing the requested books. The service, called Books on Demand, began in January 2000. An analysis of the requests at the end of the first two years of service indicated that these patron-selected books were more likely to have repeat circulations than the books acquired through normal collection development processes. When the program reached its tenth year, the authors analyzed and compared the books purchased through Books on Demand with all other purchased books during the same period. Findings indicate that books acquired through this user-initiated program have higher circulation rates than books acquired through the normal selection channels. The difference is quite large, a mean of 4.1 compared to a mean of 2.4, when the first interlibrary loan use is included as a circulation. Therefore, the authors recommend that libraries investigate a service of purchasing books requested via interlibrary loan as a complement to other collection development efforts.

INTRODUCTION AND BACKGROUND

Do books purchased on the basis of patron interlibrary loan (ILL) requests circulate more than those purchased by normal collection development methods? Does the status of the requesting patron affect the future circulation of a book? Do books in some call number ranges circulate more than others? These are the research questions that have been on the minds of librarians since libraries started purchasing a substantial number of patron-requested titles.

The Purdue University Libraries implemented a patron-driven book selection service, called Books on Demand, in January 2000, buying—instead of borrowing—recently published English-language scholarly books submitted as ILL requests by faculty, graduate students, and undergraduates. In 2002, several Purdue librarians analyzed about half the books purchased during the program's first two years and concluded that the Books on Demand program was a valuable complement to collection development activities and consistently added relevant scholarly titles to the collection. This conclusion was based on bibliographers' assessment of the appropriateness of the 800 titles. This study was repeated in 2009 and is published as a companion to this article.[1]

However, another measure of the success of the Books on Demand program would be to compare circulation trends with those of books purchased by the normal collection development process. Circulation of a book is one measure of the importance of the book to the collection. Books that are never taken from the shelf, regardless of their inherent quality, are not useful to the collection. The goal of the collection development librarian is to select books that users will want to read. This is an art, not a science. There is no way to know in advance whether a book will be checked out and read by a user. Therefore, another way of assessing the value to the collection of the Books on Demand titles would be to compare their circulation records with books acquired through normal selection methods.

Although circulation data were not a focus of the earlier study, there was some indication that the Books on Demand titles added to the Humanities, Social Science, and Education (HSSE) Library and to the Management & Economics Library were potentially high circulators.

> ... Subsequent circulation figures show that 68% of the Books on Demand titles acquired during the project's first two years have circulated at least once after the initial use by the original ILL patron (42% have circulated more than once); in contrast, 36% of titles normally acquired during the same time period for the HSSE Library have circulated at least once (16% have circulated more than once). Figures for the Management Library are even more dramatic: all Books on Demand titles had at least one checkout, whereas only 48% of the books selected and purchased with library funds had circulated one or more times during the same two years. (Anderson et al. 2002)

In 2002, these indications of high circulation were viewed cautiously, as it was very early in the service and many books had not been on the shelf long enough for circulation trends to influence decision making on whether the program was successful. Also, patron-initiated requests are for a specific and immediate research need, so initially the books indicated higher circulation because each Books on Demand title started with one circulation. Would they continue to show higher circulation? If so, this would add to the support for the program as did the bibliographers' assessment.

Books selected by librarians or via the approval plan are purchased with long-term objectives, for the bibliographers' responsibility is to build a collection that meets the *current and future* needs of *all* students and researchers. The bibliographers select books identified by the approval vendor and from publishers' catalogs. They often develop relationships with faculty members so that they understand their research interests, and they often encourage faculty members to send them requests. All this takes professional time. Some librarians have suggested that time spent on collection development could be used in other services, if libraries simply ordered the books users request, either through ILL or through catalog records for print or electronic books that meet the libraries' subject profile. The argument is that the books requested by users circulate more than those selected by librarians, implying that patron requests are better selections and that simply purchasing their requests is a less labor-intensive way to build a collection. Can libraries curtail their bibliographic responsibilities? A look at the circulation trends of Books on Demand titles would help librarians make this decision. It would also help guide the determination of what percentage of our book budget to allocate to the Books on Demand program.

METHODOLOGY AND COMPILATION OF THE DATA

To investigate the circulation trends of the patron-initiated purchases, the books needed to be compared to a control group. The authors and titles for the Books on Demand program came from two sources: the Clio and ILLiad integrated library systems. The circulation data came from the *Voyager* ILS system used by the Purdue Libraries since 1998. The technical problem was to match titles from the ILL systems with titles from the *Voyager* system; eventually all but 52 titles were matched. For comparison purposes, another data set was collected for books purchased during the same time interval as the Books on Demand titles. These books were selected by librarians, obtained on approval plans, or arrived automatically as continuation orders. Gift books and reference books were excluded. Circulation data for both sets of books were obtained on September 14, 2009. For ease of reference, the authors refer to these as the Books on Demand data set and the control data set.

The Books on Demand data set contains 9,327 titles. The data for each title include author, title, publisher, date of publication, date the book was received by ILL, date the book was cataloged, the Dewey call number, the status of the requestor, the academic department of the requestor, the name of the campus library to which the book was sent, and the number of circulations of the title between the date it was cataloged and September 14, 2009. In this study the number of circulations is further segmented according to the status of the user and whether the circulations were for two-hour reserve use or for normal circulation use. The categories for the status of the requestor and the status of the user are the same: faculty, graduate student, undergraduate student, and other. The status "other" is usually staff, but occasionally includes visiting faculty.

The control data set contains 141,112 titles. Author, title, and publisher data were not collected for this data set because they were not used in the analysis. The data set does include the date the book was cataloged, the call number, and the number of circulations between that date and September 14, 2009. As in the Books on Demand data set, circulation for each control book was also categorized by the status of the user and the type of circulation, i.e., two-hour reserve or home circulation.

Certain constraints and idiosyncrasies of the data need to be noted. It is impossible to avoid data errors in such large data sets. The authors period-ically checked the data for errors and believe that the error rate is less than one-half of one percent. The first item is a definition of a *circulation*, clarify-ing what is included and when it was taken. A circulation was measured as a charge, not a discharge. The circulation numbers for the control data set are limited to the number of charges since the date of cataloging. The Books on Demand data set also contains the same circulation data, e.g., the charge numbers since the date of cataloging, but in addition each Books on Demand title had one use as an ILL item before it was cataloged. In the tables and discussions, this study clearly states whether the ILL use is included in the circulation numbers. The circulation counts include both charges for normal use and charges for in-library two-hour reserve use. Again, the discussion clearly identifies whether the results include the two-hour reserve charges. The second item is *withdrawn books*. Books that were acquired in the time interval under study but that were withdrawn were not included since there is no circulation data for them. The third item is a *clarification of the time* covered by this study. The time interval established for both data sets was books acquired between January 2000 and December 2008. These books also had to have been cataloged between January 2000 and April 2009. To have comparable data sets, the control data set time period matched the identical time interval as the Books on Demand data set. The final issue is merging Dewey classification numbers for books with Library of Congress (LC) classification. In January 2009, the Purdue Libraries switched from the Dewey classification to the Library of Congress classification schedule. Be-cause the subject analysis is based on Dewey classification, the Dewey class number for those titles classed in LC was obtained from the MARC record. However, the MARC record did not always have a Dewey class; therefore, there are 17 titles in the Books on Demand data set and 173 in the control data set without Dewey numbers, explaining why the total number of books in the tables does not match exactly.

RESULTS OF THE COMPARISON

Do Book Purchases Based on Patron Requests Circulate More Than Those Purchased by the Libraries' Normal Collection Development Methods?

The first stage of the analysis looked simply at the total average circulations for Books on Demand titles after they were cataloged compared to the control group of books purchased through normal procedures. The objective is to see how likely or unlikely it is for a book to be chosen by a user once it is on the shelves with other books on the subject. Total average circulations included all types of circulations: 3-week loans, 16-week loans, short-term loans, and reserve book loans. The Books on Demand titles circulated an average of 3.323, while the control group books circulated an average of 3.030. This first, preliminary statistic indicates that once the books are on the shelves, the Books on Demand books receive slightly more use than the normal books. Another way to visualize this statistic is to see that for every 10 circulations of Books on Demand titles, there are 9 circulations of the normal group. However, this statistic includes two-hour reserve use, which is somewhat different from the normal circulation; reserve books are extensively used by a very small group of students for two hours or less because of specific assignments. One title from the control data set had 1,375 two-hour reserve loans. Numbers like this can greatly influence the averages. *So the next question was whether reserve book circulation significantly affected the average circulation statistics.* Without the reserve data included in the calculation, Books on Demand titles show higher circulation; they circulated slightly more than three times while normal books circulated slightly fewer than two and one half times. Table 1 compares the circulation statistics after each group of books was cataloged *both with and without reserve circulation data.*

Another interesting item that Table 1 shows is that books purchased through the normal process are three times more likely to be placed on reserve as the Books on Demand titles are. This difference is not surprising, since books needed for reserve are purchased out of the normal library funds, while the Books on Demand titles are requested for an immediate research need. Normal selection methods are more successful for acquiring books needed to support the undergraduate curriculum directly.

TABLE 1 Comparison of the Circulation of Books on Demand and the Control Group Books Purchased in the Same Time Interval; Average Total, Normal, and Reserve Circulations

	Books on Demand Books: Circulation After Cataloging	Control Books: Circulation
No. of books	9,327	141,112
No. of total circulations	30,996	427,608
Average total circulations	**3.323**	**3.030**
No. of normal circulations	29,062	340,121
Average normal circulations	**3.116**	**2.410**
No. of reserve circulations	1,934	87,487
Average reserve circulations	**0.207**	**0.620**

How Are the Statistics Affected When the ILL Use Is Added as the First Circulation Count?

Books on Demand titles have already had one circulation before cataloging. Table 2 includes the circulation rate both with and without that first circulation counted. These statistics do not include reserve circulation data. Adding the ILL use to the Books on Demand circulation statistics increases the books' average circulation to 4.114, compared to 2.410 for normal books. Once the data are adjusted by removing the reserve circulation and adding the ILL circulation, the Books on Demand titles circulate significantly more than normal books.

What Percentage of the Books Never Circulate *After* They Are on the Shelves?

Many proponents of user-initiated collection development cite the high percentage of books purchased through normal selection methods that never circulate. These are the true shelf-sitters; they may remain on the library shelves for years and never be moved unless the collection is shifted. The 1970s Pittsburgh study, for example, reported zero circulation for 39.8% of its collection after six years on the shelf (Bulick et al. 1979). With currently declining circulations, a rate of 50% would not be an unreasonable estimate

TABLE 2 Circulation Rates for Books on Demand (BoD) Both with and without the First Circulation Counted and for Control Books

	BoD Books: Circulation by Interlibrary Loan	BoD Books: Circulation After cataloging	BoD Books: Total Circulation	Control books
No. of books	9,327	9,327	9,327	141,112
Average circulation	1.000	3.116	4.116	2.410
No. of circulations	9,327	29,062	38,389	340,121

TABLE 3 Number and Percentage of Books for Each Level of Circulation (Zero Circulations Are Books That Are Shelf-Sitters)

Books on Demand Books			Control Books		
No. of Circulations	No. of Books	Percentage of Books	No. of Circulations	No. of Books	Percentage of Books
0	1,722	18.46	0	46,996	33.30
1	2,164	23.20	1	31,829	22.56
2	1,578	16.92	2	19,580	13.88
3	1,148	12.31	3	12,426	8.81
4	709	7.60	4	8,094	5.74
5	485	5.20	5	5,503	3.90
6	365	3.91	6	3,914	2.77
7	257	2.76	7	2,858	2.03
8	195	2.09	8	2,116	1.50
9	153	1.64	9	1,534	1.09
10	118	1.27	10	1,161	0.82

for today's research collections. So the next probe was to determine the percentage of books acquired through Books on Demand that were shelf-sitters and compare this percentage with the percentage of control books with no circulation. The Books on Demand titles show a lower rate of shelf-sitters (18%) compared to the rate for regular books (33%). Table 3 indicates that overall the Books on Demand titles outperform the control books.

Does the Heavier Use of Books on Demand Titles Include All Types of Patrons?

In 2008/2009, the number of faculty members at the West Lafayette Purdue campus was 3,038, while the number of graduate students was 7,427 (Purdue University 2009). The combined group of faculty and graduate students is Purdue's researchers; so graduate students constitute 70% of the researchers. The undergraduate student count was 31,761. Table 4 shows that both faculty and graduate student use the Books on Demand titles at about a 50% higher rate than the control titles, even with the ILL use excluded. Undergraduates, on the other hand, used both the Books on Demand and the control titles at about the same rate. Table 4 also shows that graduate students are certainly the heaviest users of both Books on Demand titles and the control titles.

Does the Status of the Requesting Patron Affect the Future Circulation of a Book?

Books requested by undergraduates had the highest average circulation, while those requested by faculty had the lowest average circulation. This

TABLE 4 Circulation Rates by Patron Status for Books on Demand and Control Books

	Books on Demand Books: Circulation After Cataloging	Control Books
No. of books	**9,327**	**141,112**
No. of faculty circulations	3,109	32,500
Average faculty circulation	**0.333**	0.230
No. of graduate student circulations	14,080	136,016
Average graduate student circulation	**1.510**	0.964
No. of undergraduate circulations	7,392	116,988
Average undergraduate circulation	0.793	0.829
No. of other circulations	4,481	54,617
Average other circulation	**0.480**	0.387
No. of total circulations	29,062	340,121
Average total circulation	**3.116**	**2.410**

conclusion is shown in the last column in Table 5. It shows the average circulation of Books on Demand books based on the status of the patron who requested the book from ILL. The initial ILL use is not included in the average circulations, nor is the two-hour reserve use.

The four columns to the left of the total column show how frequently the various categories of borrowers used the books requested by the faculty, graduate students, and undergraduate students. The four columns show that faculty members are more likely to borrow books requested by faculty, graduate students are more likely to borrow books requested by graduate students, etc. Not surprisingly, faculty made little use of books requested by undergraduates. On the other hand, although undergraduates are most likely to use books requested by undergraduates, they made as much use of faculty selections as they did of graduate student selections. Graduate students made the heaviest use of titles requested by every category of patron except undergraduates.

It could be argued that the results in Table 5 are due to the fact that the patron who first charges the book after it is cataloged is the often same one

TABLE 5 Circulation Rates of Books on Demand Titles by Requesting Patron Status (Circulation Rates Are Calculated after Cataloging; Data Exclude Interlibrary Loan [ILL] Use)

Books Requested From ILL by Status of Requestor		Average Circulation of Books on Demand Books after Cataloging by Status of Patron Borrowing the Book				
ILL Requestor	No. of Books Requested	Faculty	Graduates	Undergraduates	Other	Total
Faculty	2,366	**0.51**	1.00	0.69	0.40	2.60
Graduates	5,589	0.28	**1.83**	0.69	0.46	3.27
Undergraduates	704	0.19	1.02	**1.84**	0.57	3.62
Other	668	0.28	1.12	0.91	**0.85**	3.16
Total	9,327	0.33	1.51	0.79	0.48	3.12

who originally used it as an ILL loan. For that reason, the authors removed the first circulation after ILL use and recalculated the averages. The results were very similar, especially for graduate and undergraduate students.

Does the Subject Classification of the Requested Book Affect Its Circulation Rate?

Table 6 shows that the average circulation for Books on Demand titles requested by faculty shows little difference by Dewey class number. Those requested by graduate students and by undergraduates show more variability by Dewey number. By cross-comparing the tables, it can be seen that average circulation for history titles (Dewey 900s) is about the same for each category of patron. On the other hand, general titles (Dewey 000s) requested by graduate and undergraduate students had much higher circulation than did those requested by faculty.

The most significant finding of Table 6 is that science and technology titles (Dewey 500s and 600s) had high mean circulation rates irrespective of which category of patron requested them. Science and technology titles requested by graduate and undergraduate students had slightly higher circulation than did those requested by the faculty. This fact is even more interesting to note realizing that the Books on Demand service is very heavily used by liberal arts patrons compared to science and technology patrons (82% of the Books on Demand titles fall into liberal arts call number ranges; only 13% fall into the science/technology ranges).

TABLE 6 Mean Circulation Rates of Books on Demand by Dewey Classification and Status of Requestor (17 Titles Are Missing from the Dewey Tables; Total Mean Circulation Includes ILL Use; Subtract 1 from Any Mean Circulation to Remove ILL Use)

Faculty Requests			Graduate Requests			Undergraduate Requests		
Dewey No.	No. of Books	Total Mean Circulation	Dewey No.	No. of Books	Total Mean Circulation	Dewey No.	No. of Books	Total Mean Circulation
000s	93	3.09	000s	232	6.06	000s	52	7.35
100s	137	3.80	100s	425	3.95	100s	27	5.74
200s	102	2.86	200s	307	3.12	200s	44	3.95
300s	785	3.72	300s	1,968	4.16	300s	214	4.19
400s	63	3.76	400s	171	5.12	400s	8	2.75
500s	**121**	**4.16**	**500s**	**242**	**6.08**	**500s**	**19**	**8.00**
600s	**215**	**4.06**	**600s**	**691**	**5.14**	**600s**	**123**	**5.24**
700s	256	3.53	700s	347	4.12	700s	76	4.49
800s	248	3.75	800s	708	3.80	800s	41	3.73
900s	344	3.02	900s	485	3.24	900s	99	3.35
TOTAL	2,364			5,576			703	

CONCLUSIONS

Books acquired through a program such as the Books on Demand service offered by the Purdue University Libraries ILL department have higher circulation rates than books acquired through the normal selection channels. The difference is quite large, 4.1 compared to 2.4, when the first ILL use is included as a circulation and reserve uses are excluded. The difference is smaller, 3.1 compared to 2.4, when the first use is not included. This result confirms the conclusions of the 2002 study of Purdue's Books on Demand service (Anderson et al. 2002).

From a practical standpoint, these results mean that academic libraries are well advised to acquire recent English-language books of a scholarly nature when they are requested through ILL. This analysis of the subsequent circulation trends along with the bibliographers' analysis of the appropriateness of the books users request has led to a continuation and expansion of the Books on Demand program at Purdue University. Over the past 10 years, we have allocated about 5.5% of the book allocation. The librarians involved in this assessment are recommending an increase to 10% of the allocation. The next step beyond this practice would be the acquisition of patron-requested books that are not ILL requests. For example, the library could load records for print or electronic books into the OPAC that match the Libraries' approval plan profile and then order the titles that patrons select. If the Purdue Libraries were to do this, one would expect the resulting mean circulation for a comparable time period to be between 3.1 and 4.1. Some books selected from the OPAC would be for immediate use, as in the ILL case; one would expect them to average around 4.1 circulations per book. Other books would not be for immediate use; one would expect their average to be about 3.1. Other academic libraries would no doubt have different upper and lower bounds. Moving to a patron-driven book selection model of this type does entail the possibility of declining returns to scale. This could happen if faculty selected large numbers of books from the OPAC to build the library collection rather than to acquire books they personally need. The average circulation of Books on Demand books selected by faculty was 2.6 after cataloging, i.e., less than the lower bound of 3.1. The acquisition of many books in this manner would lead to a decline in mean circulation.

For a program of patron selection to be successful for all users, it is important to have input from all constituencies on campus. At first glance, the data in this study seem to indicate that students make better selectors than faculty, since the circulation rates for books requested by graduate and undergraduate students are higher than the rates for books requested by members of the faculty. Graduate students are the heaviest users of monographs and the heaviest users of the Books on Demand service, and their selections have some appeal to both undergraduates and faculty. It is important to note that this study also shows that faculty are the most frequent users of books requested by faculty and they make only minor use of the books requested by graduate and undergraduate students. Therefore, it appears that the reading needs of faculty can best be determined by other faculty.

There does seem to be some variation in circulation rates of patron-requested books based on subject matter. There is further variation when one takes into account whether it is students or faculty members who requested the books in the various subjects. In a collection development policy, it might be difficult to even out these differences; it may, in fact, not even be desirable. Other factors, such as major strengths of the academic institution in teaching and research, might actually favor disparities of this nature. Knowledge of this type, however, does give the collection development team one more tool for crafting a good collection policy.

ACKNOWLEDGEMENT

The authors gratefully acknowledge Amy Winks for extracting the raw data from the Clio and ILLiad databases.

NOTE

1. A follow-up of this 2002 study is published in this journal issue. (See Anderson et al. 2010).

REFERENCES

Anderson, Kristine J., Robert S. Freeman, Jean-Pierre V. M. Hérubel, Lawrence J. Mykytiuk, Judith M. Nixon, and Suzanne M. Ward. 2002. Buy, don't borrow: Bibliographers' analysis of academic library collection development through interlibrary loan requests. *Collection Management* 27(3/4): 1–10.

Anderson, Kristine J., Robert S. Freeman, Jean-Pierre V. M. Hérubel, Lawrence J. Mykytiuk, Judith M. Nixon, and Suzanne M. Ward. 2010. *Liberal arts Books on Demand: A decade of patron-driven collection development, Part 1.* Collection Management 35(3/4): 125–141.

Bulick, Stephen, William N. Sabor, and Roger Flynn. 1979. Circulation and in-house use of books. In *Use of library materials: The University of Pittsburgh study*, ed. Allen Kent, 9–55. New York: Marcel Dekker.

Purdue University, Office of Institutional Research. 2009. *Purdue University data digest: Enrollment by college/school and by student level—West Lafayette campus (for fall semester in academic years 1998–99 through 2007–08)* [cited 11-09-2009 2009]. Available from http://www.purdue.edu/datadigest/2007-08/pages/students/stu_sch_level.htm.

Just How Right Are the Customers? An Analysis of the Relative Performance of Patron-Initiated Interlibrary Loan Monograph Purchases

DAVID C. TYLER, YANG XU, JOYCE C. MELVIN, MARYLOU EPP, and ANITA M. KREPS

University of Nebraska-Lincoln, Lincoln, Nebraska

There has been a flurry of interest in programs for collection development through patron-initiated requests. However, some librarians have been concerned that such methods run the risk of producing idiosyncratic collections with poor usage and poor use value. The University of Nebraska-Lincoln Libraries have operated such a program through the Interlibrary Loan Department over a five-year period. The following study assesses the relative performance of the program's interlibrary loan–acquired monographs in terms of prices paid per rates of annual circulation, relative use at the topical level, and annual rates of circulation.

INTRODUCTION

To meet their patrons' needs, many libraries have started purchasing selected books requested through interlibrary loan (ILL). When discussing such a program, however, the authors have found some academic librarians to be slightly wary. Librarians' concerns largely center upon governance of the collection as expressed in collection development policies, librarians' knowledge of what departments and colleges will require, and university documents detailing current and future campus priorities. Librarians worry that patrons know little and care less for such things and are interested solely in meeting their own immediate needs. Collection development driven by patron requests, therefore, runs the risk of producing a collection of idiosyncratic materials that could see little use and would, therefore, have an ineffective, or poor, use value (Comer and Lorenzen 2006).

BACKGROUND

Over five fiscal years (2003/2004 to 2007/2008), the University of Nebraska-Lincoln (UNL) University Libraries has managed a small purchase-on-demand program through its ILL department on a continuing trial basis. The UNL University Libraries include the Don L. Love Memorial Library and six branch libraries, which, together with the Marvin and Virginia Schmid Law Library, house roughly three million print volumes and maintain over 44,000 current serial subscriptions (University of Nebraska-Lincoln Libraries 2009a).[1] The UNL Libraries' ILL department is a vital part of the libraries' access services and, during the trial period, handled an average of 50,902 ILL borrowing and lending transactions per year (University of Nebraska-Lincoln Libraries 2009b). The UNL Libraries' ILL purchase-on-demand program was co-initiated by the ILL department and the Collection Development Committee and implemented at the beginning of the 2003 fiscal year. As was the case with the many similar programs that have been reported in the literature, the UNL program adopted some guidelines to ensure that materials requested through the program would be suitable. For example, there was a cost ceiling (initially $75 and currently $175); books had to be published within the last three years; exclusions include undergraduate-level textbooks, popular-interest books, computer or lab manuals, fiction, plays, and poetry; and so forth. The UNL University Libraries have historically purchased books for the circulating collection via one of four channels: approval plans; librarians' firm orders; donor bequests (in essence, approval plan–style orders paid for with targeted donated funds); and lost book replacement orders. To these, the ILL program added a fifth option: book orders placed via patron-initiated ILL requests, which amounted to 2.1% of books acquired and 2.4% of spending during the five-year trial period.

To assess the impact and relative performance of the ILL-acquired books, the authors queried the online catalog in December 2008 for a list of all books available for circulation that had been acquired and made available for checkout during the trial period. Table 1 shows that approval plan books and librarians' firm orders made up the overwhelming bulk of acquisitions. As expected, given past research on library circulation, the authors discovered that only a slight majority of the materials had circulated at least once. Figure 1 shows that just over 46% of books had not yet circulated, 26% had circulated once, 13% had circulated twice, and the remaining 15% had circulated three or more times (note: throughout the study, percentages have been rounded

TABLE 1 UNL University Libraries: General Characteristics of Recent Acquisitions

	2003/2004	2004/2005	2005/2006	2006/2007	2007/2008	Totals
Volumes acquired	16,978	15,228	16,408	13,907	7,420	69,941
Approval plan	8,664	7,814	8,274	7,289	4,581	36,622
Firm orders	6,717	6,666	7,243	5,945	2,344	28,915
Donor bequests	522	418	442	282	205	1,869
Lost book	743	28	160	74	79	1,084
Patron-initiated ILL	332	302	289	317	211	1,451
Total spending	$805,108.55	$739,377.35	$864,361.41	$710,002.44	$380,412.37	$3,499, 262.12
Approval plan	$428,634.09	$382,081.26	$417,248.36	$365,113.81	$229,206.43	$1,822, 283.95
Firm orders	$315,347.74	$325,664.96	$405,110.52	$308,740.91	$131,189.85	$1,486, 053.98
Donor bequests	$17,466.84	$13,149.75	$13,699.55	$12,458.26	$6,629.74	$63,404.14
Lost book	$24,402.95	$1,386.23	$10,718.78	$3,977.13	$3,417.41	$43,902.50
Patron-initiated ILL	$19,256.93	$17,095.15	$17,584.20	$19,712.33	$9,968.94	$83,617.55
Total circulations (2003–2008)	29,295	21,612	18,252	11,946	4,136	85,241
Approval plan	13,426	9,768	8,074	5,357	2,097	38,722
Firm orders	12,967	10,552	8,972	5,737	1,520	39,748
Donor bequests	273	230	134	86	66	789
Lost book	1,279	59	204	82	86	1,710
Patron-initiated ILL	1,350	1,003	868	684	367	4,272

Note. The decrease in firm ordering in 2006–2008 may be largely attributed to budgetary constraints. The decrease in approval plan acquisitions may in part be attributed to a switch in vendors in the middle of the 2006/2007 fiscal year and the implementation of a more restrictive approval plan.

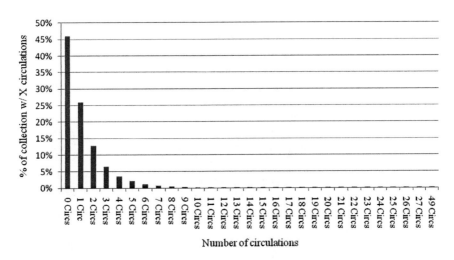

FIGURE 1 Circulation frequencies for all recent acquisitions, 2003/2004–2007/2008.

to the nearest whole or one-tenth of one percent, and other reported values have been rounded to no more than three decimal places).

ANALYSIS OF ILL REQUESTS

Several earlier studies indicated that at larger institutions, graduate students or faculty made most of the filled purchase requests and that most of these requests came from patrons affiliated with the arts and humanities or the social sciences (Anderson et al. 2002; Ward 2002; Bombeld and Hanerfeld 2004; Houle 2004; Foss 2007; Way 2009). Figures 2a and 2b reveal that the filled requests of the UNL Libraries' program appear to be fairly typical: graduate students and faculty members made 74% of filled requests; arts and humanities and social science affiliates made 66.4% of filled requests.[2]

ANALYSIS OF RECENT ACQUISITIONS' PERFORMANCE

Thus, it would seem that the UNL University Libraries' ILL purchase-on-demand program has been fairly typical. The relative size of the ILL program's budget, the behavior of the collection where circulation is concerned, and the pattern of patron requests all seem to be fairly closely in accord with the experiences and results reported by others. Although librarians at UNL have been pleased with the program, there have been concerns that ILL acquisitions could have poorer use value because of potentially higher prices paid for the books (approval and firm-ordered books come with discounted pricing) and because of their potential to be on topics of limited interest.

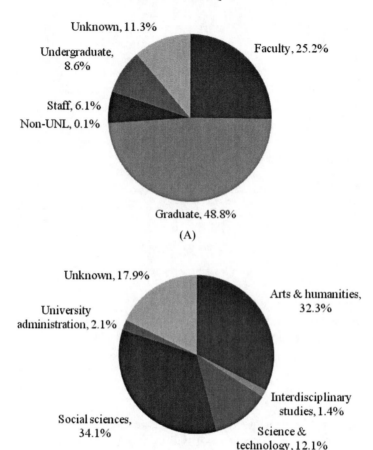

PATRON-DRIVEN ACQUISITIONS

(A)

(B)

FIGURE 2 Percentage of interlibrary loan purchases by patron type (panel A) and by disciplinary affiliation (panel B).

Colleagues have also expressed doubts as to whether ILL purchases really circulate significantly more than do books purchased through traditional channels. To address these concerns, the authors will assess the short-term performance of UNL's ILL purchase-on-demand books against the performance of books added concurrently to the circulating collection via traditional means.

Effective Use Value

To address the issue of effective use value (see the Appendix for definition), the authors decided first to calculate the average stock turnover rates (see the Appendix for definition) of the recently acquired books as a whole, of the books acquired via traditional means, and of the books acquired via the

ILL program and to employ these rates as a measure of use (note: in-house use had not been collected) (Baker and Wallace 2002). The authors found the average stock turnover rate for all of the recently acquired books to be approximately 0.42 circulations, or nearly one circulation every 2.4 years. To determine how relatively cost-effective these recent book purchases had been, the authors then attempted to calculate the resultant average cost of an annual circulation, or the use value (see Appendix) (Cohen and Kern 1979). Unfortunately, data for the UNL Libraries' fixed costs (e.g., administration, maintenance, storage, and opportunity costs) and for total variable costs (i.e., all costs related to ordering and acquisition) had not been collected. Thus, the authors employed the data that were available: the prices paid for the books. So, to summarize, the question was as follows: what, in effect, was the average price of an annual circulation for the UNL Libraries' recent acquisitions, given the total amount paid for the books and their total calculated stock turnover? For the 69,941 recently acquired books, the library paid an average of $50.03 per book and had an average use value ratio of $119.83:1 annual circulation.[3]

Before comparing the use values of ILL-acquired and traditionally acquired books, the authors elected first to reduce the data set to only those Library of Congress (LC) subclasses with both ILL and traditional acquisitions with calculable values.[4] These adjustments left 64,732 traditionally acquired books (94.5% of traditionally acquired books) and 1,445 ILL-acquired books (99.6% of ILL-acquired books) in 134 LC subclasses. The authors repeated the calculations above for the traditionally acquired books and found that they had a stock turnover rate of 0.41, an average price of $49.99, and a resultant average use value ratio of $122.34:1 annual circulation. Similarly, the ILL-acquired books had a stock turnover rate, average price, and an average use value ratio of 1.05, $57.63, and $54.99:1 annual circulation, respectively. When the authors compared the head-to-head performance of the books grouped into each of their 134 LC subclasses, they found that ILL-acquired books had more effective average use value ratios in 119 (89%) of the subclasses. It should be noted that this favorable imbalance occurred despite traditionally acquired books' having lower average prices paid in 85 subclasses.[5]

An objection raised to the above approach was that the purchase-on-demand and traditional acquisition represent two different modes of acquisition with different purposes and that the ILL books have an inherent advantage in that they were guaranteed at least one circulation upon acquisition, while traditionally acquired books must wait on the shelves to be discovered. Partly to rectify this imbalance, the authors repeated the above assessment but included only those traditionally acquired books that had circulated. This recalculation reduced the number of traditionally acquired books to 34,604. These books' average price was $48.88, and their stock turnover rate was approximately 0.76, which was still well below the ILL books' rate. Their resultant average use value ratio proved to be $63.92:1 annual circulation, which was also slightly worse than the ILL-acquired books' use value. When comparing the grouped acquisitions against one another in their LC subclasses, the authors found that ILL books outperformed traditionally acquired books in 83 of the 134 LC subclasses. So, even after removing the main handicap for traditional avenues for library acquisition, ILL-acquired books still provided comparable and perhaps even slightly more effective use value where prices paid and stock turnover rates were concerned.

Topical Idiosyncrasy

To address the issue of potential topical idiosyncrasy (see Appendix), the authors examined into which LC subclasses the ILL purchase-on-demand program's acquisitions fell and then assessed the relative performance of these subclasses by comparing them to the average relative use factors (see Appendix) of the 257 LC subclasses that had had collection acquisitions during the interval. The expectation underlying these calculations was that the use and holdings of each LC subclass should be proportional; if discrepancies between proportional use and holdings were discovered, then the LC subclass(es) in question would have been either relatively underutilized or overutilized (Bonn 1974; Mills 1982). For the assessment, the authors elected to use Mills' percentage expected use rather than a simple ratio of use to holdings because most readers will find percentages easier to read. Also, rather than calculate merely a circulations-to-holdings ratio to identify the subclasses with the greatest relative circulation, the authors also calculated a volume-use-to-holdings ratio to discover how well distributed across the purchased books the circulations were within each LC subclass. The circulation-based metric will provide a relative indicator of how much the books in an LC subclass had circulated. The volume use–based metric should provide a relative indicator of how widely distributed circulation activity was across all of the books in an LC subclass.

In the resultant scatter graph (Figure 3), the intersection of the figure represents the average of averages for the 257 LC subclasses that had acquisitions during the interval. The plotted points show the relative performance of the 140 LC subclasses that had ILL acquisitions. Subclasses plotted in the large upper right-hand quadrant (henceforth Q1) experienced higher than average stock turnover rates and had a higher than average percentage of books circulate. In other words, the books were checked out comparatively often, and the checkouts were spread across a better-than-average number of books. Subclasses plotted in the lower right-hand quadrant (Q2) experienced higher than average stock turnover rates, but that turnover was concentrated in a lower than average percentage of books. Subclasses plotted in the upper left-hand quadrant (Q3) experienced lower than average stock

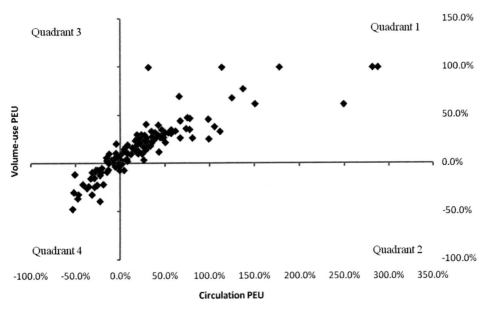

FIGURE 3 Percentage expected use (PEU) of Library of Congress subclasses with interlibrary loan purchases relative to the collection average of averages.

turnover rates, but a higher than average percentage of books were circulated. Last, subclasses plotted in the lower left-hand quadrant (Q4) experienced lower than average stock turnover rates and relatively less book use.

As Figure 3 shows, roughly 61.4% of the LC subclasses with ILL acquisitions fell into Q1, 1.4% fell into Q2, 12.9% fell into Q3, and 24.3% fell into Q4, the least desirable of the quadrants. What was perhaps most impressive about these results was not their distribution, which did reflect very favorably on the ILL program, but the composition of the quadrants. The LC subclasses in Q1 accounted for 77.1% of the books acquired via the ILL program and 76.1% of the monies spent. The LC subclasses in the slightly less desirable Q2 (1.2% acquisitions; 2.0% spending) and Q3 (12.5%; 10.8%) accounted for just over half of the remainder, and ILL acquisitions in Q4 (9.2%; 11.2%) accounted for just under half of the remainder. Thus, roughly 90.8% of ILL acquisitions and 88.9% of the program's spending fell into quadrants with above-average use of some sort, and most of those acquisitions fell into the relatively high-circulation/high–volume use Q1. While this method cannot address the utility of any particular book ordered, it does illustrate that the library's patrons did an excellent job of ordering titles that fell within the higher-use and more mainstream topical areas of the collection, as defined by LC subclass, and of avoiding excessive additions to more topically remote and little-used areas. Selection guidelines may also have influenced the fact that more mainstream titles were purchased. Nevertheless, with some guiding parameters in place, library patrons appear to do well at selecting topically appropriate books for the collection. This conclusion follows conclusions in other studies (Anderson et al. 2002; Ward et al. 2003; Chan 2004; Ruppel 2006; Way 2009).

Circulation Performance

Last, to address the issue of potentially significant differences in amounts and rates of circulation, the authors, following the lead of earlier studies, assessed what percentage of the books of each order type had zero, one, or more total circulations. Several studies had indicated that the books purchased via ILL purchase-on-demand circulated more than did items acquired by traditional means and that such books were more likely to have circulated multiple times (Perdue and Van Fleet 1999; Anderson et al. 2002; Ward 2002; Allen et al. 2003; Ward et al. 2003; Bombeld and Hanerfeld 2004; Brug and MacWaters 2004; Chan 2004; Houle 2004; Campbell 2006; Zopfi-Jordan 2008; Way 2009). The books purchased through the UNL Libraries' program appear to have followed the general trend, as Figure 4 illustrates. Sizeable percentages of the books acquired via traditional channels had not circulated at the time data collection was completed, while only 1.3% of the ILL purchases had zero recorded circulations (i.e., the books were requested but never picked up).[6] Also, much larger percentages of the ILL-acquired books had experienced multiple circulations.

This simple figure, while intuitively persuasive, does not, of course, establish that there were statistically significant differences in performance among the five avenues of acquisition where stock turnover rates were concerned. Before testing for differences, the authors tested for the normality of the data and for other proper distributions and found UNL's data not to be normal, log normal, Weibull, or gamma, so the authors turned to non-parametric methods and, as there were one nominal and one measurement

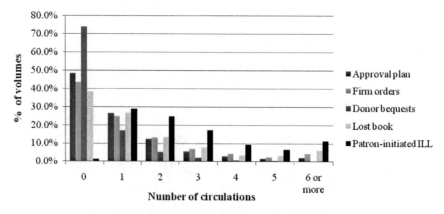

FIGURE 4 Number of circulations by order type.

TABLE 2 Acquisition Types by Annual Stock Turnover Rate (All Acquisitions)

Analysis Variable: Annual Stock Turnover					
Acquisition Type	Volumes	Mean	SD	Minimum	Maximum
Approval plan	36,622	0.363	0.571	0	12.0
Firm orders	28,915	0.470	0.720	0	13.067
Donor bequests	1,869	0.154	0.385	0	4.8
Lost book	1,084	0.461	0.697	0	7.636
ILL	1,451	1.047	0.763	0	6.486

Wilcoxon Scores (Rank Sums) for Variable Annual Stock Turnover (by Acquisition Type)					
Acquisition Type	Volumes	Sum of Scores	Expected Under H_0	SD Under H_0	Mean Score
Approval plan	36,622	1,230,199,244	1,280,707,962	2,533,004.41	33,591.809
Firm orders	28,915	1,049,273,800	1,011,186,465	2,497,526.61	36,288.217
Donor bequests	1,869	45,149,837.5	65,360,799	817,914.38	24,157.216
Lost book	1,084	39,810,624.5	37,908,564	626,480.6	36,725.668
ILL	1,451	81,473,205.5	50,742,921	722,880.03	56,149.694

Kruskal-Wallis Test	
Chi-square	2698.880
DF	4
Pr > Chi-square	<.0001

Note. Average scores were used for ties.

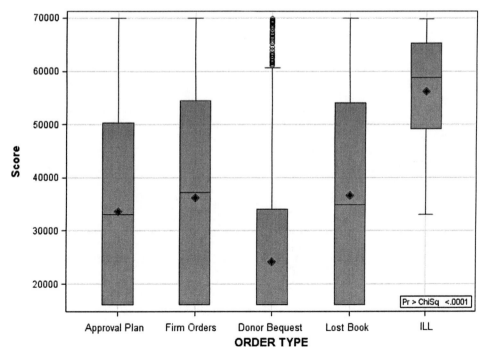

FIGURE 5 Distribution of Wilcoxon scores for annual turnover rates (all acquisitions).

TABLE 3 Acquisition Types by Annual Stock Turnover Rate (LC Subclasses with ILL Acquisitions Only)

Acquisition Type	Volumes	Mean	SD	Minimum	Maximum
		Analysis Variable: Annual Stock Turnover			
Approval plan	35,460	0.366	0.573	0	12.0
Firm orders	27,014	0.477	0.725	0	13.067
Donor bequests	1,458	0.167	0.396	0	3.6
Lost book	1,016	0.460	0.679	0	7.636
ILL	1,448	1.047	0.763	0	6.486

Acquisition Type	Volumes	Sum of scores	Expected Under H_0	SD Under H_0	Mean Score
		Wilcoxon Scores (Rank Sums) for Variable Annual Stock Turnover (by Acquisition Type)			
Approval plan	35,460	1,126,712,796	1,177,218,810	2,344,579.14	31,774.191
Firm orders	27,014	931,389,798	896,824,279	2,308,908.83	34,478.041
Donor bequests	1,458	33,771,600	48,403,413	688,797.67	23,162.963
Lost book	1,016	35,470,114	33,729,676	576,942.81	34,911.530
ILL	1,448	76,903,298	48,071,428	686,484.32	53,110.012

Kruskal-Wallis Test	
Chi-square	2524.914
DF	4
Pr > Chi-square	<.0001

Note. Average scores were used for ties.

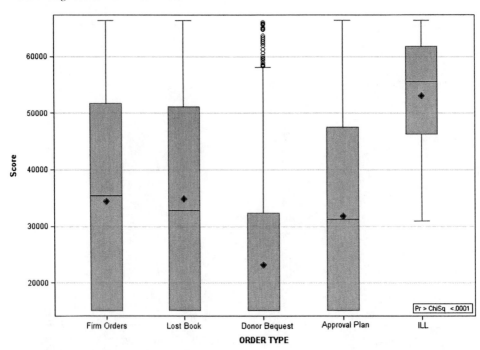

FIGURE 6 Distribution of Wilcoxon scores for annual turnover rates (LC subclasses with ILL acquisitions).

TABLE 4 Acquisition Types by Annual Stock Turnover Rate (Circulated Volumes)

Analysis Variable: Annual Stock Turnover					
Acquisition Type	Volumes	Mean	SD	Minimum	Maximum
Approval plan	18,343	0.707	0.627	0.185	12.0
Firm orders	15,242	0.838	0.787	0.185	13.067
Donor bequests	385	0.632	0.548	0.185	3.60
Lost book	634	0.732	0.730	0.185	7.636
ILL	1,427	1.061	0.759	0.194	6.486

Wilcoxon scores (rank sums) for variable annual stock turnover (by acquisition type)					
Acquisition Type	Volumes	Sum of scores	Expected Under H_0	SD under H_0	Mean score
Approval plan	18,343	311,956,514	330,467,488	986,974.932	17,006.843
Firm orders	15,242	287,634,502	274,599,872	975,369.908	18,871.178
Donor bequests	385	5,898,871.5	6,936,160	202,986.587	15,321.744
Lost book	634	10,385,498.5	11,422,144	259,572.949	16,380.913
ILL	1,427	33,259,111	25,708,832	385,040.766	23,307.015

Kruskal-Wallis Test	
Chi-square	686.514
DF	4
Pr > Chi-square	<.0001

Note. Average scores were used for ties.

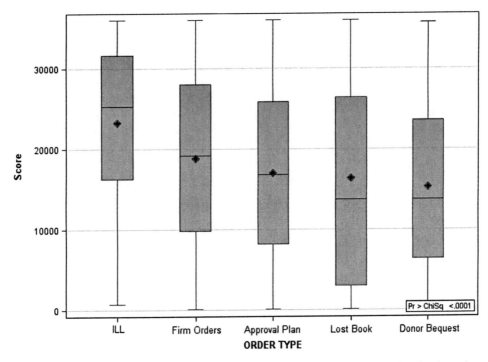

FIGURE 7 Distribution of Wilcoxon scores for annual turnover rates (circulated volumes).

value and samples with similar shapes of distribution, performed the Kruskal-Wallis test (see Appendix) on the full data set (69,941 books in 257 LC subclasses). The test showed that when the five order types' books' annual turnover rates were compared, ILL purchasing had the highest stock turnover rates on average, donor bequests had the lowest, and there was definitely a significant difference among the five types (for values, see Table 2). For a graphical, more intuitively readable representation of the order types' performance, see Figure 5. In this Wilcoxon box plot, the gray bar represents the range between each order type's 25th and 75th percentiles, the dot represents the median score, and the bisecting segment line represents the mean score. The superiority of ILL acquisition's performance should be evident.

As was the case in the section on use value, the authors were cognizant that there could be some effects related to the LC subclasses without ILL purchases that could affect the results of the analysis, so, once again, the authors reduced the data set to the subset of LC subclasses that had had both ILL and other types of purchases (137 LC subclasses; 66,396 books) and repeated the Kruskal-Wallis test. The test once again revealed that there were significant differences among the five modes of acquisition and that ILL acquisition was, again, far and away the best performer (for values, see Table 3). This difference in performance is graphically represented in Figure 6.

To answer again the objection that ILL acquisitions unfairly begin their careers in the collection with a circulation advantage, the authors repeated the test a third time, this time further reducing the set of books by removing all books with zero circulations (134 LC subclasses; 36,031 books). The authors found that, even with their advantage in the circulation sweepstakes removed, the ILL-purchased books' stock turnover rates generally outperformed those of the other four order types (for values, see Table 4). While there were again differences between the five order types' performance, Figure 7 illustrates that the performance means and medians were much nearer to one another across acquisition types and that there was considerable overlap between the acquisition types' 25th to 75th percentiles. Still, patron-initiated ILL acquisition again outperformed the other order types.[7]

CONCLUSIONS

The UNL project confirmed findings in the literature indicating that purchase-on-demand programs at libraries of several types have been very successful at obtaining cost-effective materials that are not only suitable for their collections but also meet the needs of multiple patrons. Purchase criteria, processes and workflows, and vendors have varied from program to program, but the nature and quality of the success seem remarkably consistent. In the literature, patrons and librarians have responded favorably to such programs;

several studies suggest that such services are nearly as cost-effective as ILL and lead to increased efficiencies (Perdue and Van Fleet 1999; Ward 2002; Ward et al. 2003; Bombeld and Hanerfeld 2004; Brug and MacWaters 2004; Houle 2004; Comer and Lorenzen 2006; Coopey and Snowman 2006; Foss 2007). At the UNL Libraries, the books acquired via ILL purchase-on-demand seem largely to exhibit better use value as calculated. With guidelines in place to govern the appropriateness of the books acquired, UNL library patrons have done very well at selecting books topically suitable to the collection in that the great bulk of the books purchased fell within locally high-use LC subclasses. Last, and most important, the patron-requested books circulate at higher rates and experience elevated amounts of repeat circulation. If a library's purpose is, at least in part, to obtain items that patrons will want to borrow, then a purchase-on-demand program of some sort should be treated as a necessity, for such a program seemingly guarantees that its purchases will be relatively heavily used.

LIMITATIONS OF THE STUDY AND AREAS FOR FURTHER RESEARCH

While the authors of the study are fairly confident of their findings and conclusions, this study had several limitations. Firstly, the study was nonexperimental, was conducted ex post facto, and was conducted at a single institution that may have had unusual local characteristics, so its potential to predict future outcomes and its generalizability may be somewhat hampered. However, the authors feel that the study's practical utility as a decision-supporting tool for librarians should be acceptable. Second, this study's sample of ILL-acquired books was relatively small. It would have been preferable to have had a proportionally larger sample of ILL acquisitions so as to establish more firmly that the outsized positive results of the program were not merely the result of smaller samples' vulnerability to distortion by atypical cases. Last, this study assessed merely the short-term circulation performance of recently acquired books; statistics on in-house use were not collected. The study also left open the possibility that the results reported here could be reversed by late surges in circulations of books acquired via the approval plan and firm orders. The literature suggests that such a surge would be highly unlikely (Davidson 1943; Fussler and Simon 1969; Trueswell 1969; Bulick et al. 1979; Hardesty 1981; Eldredge 1998), but an increase in later uses could occur. Thus, the authors would suggest that studies on purchase-on-demand could benefit from a meta-analysis, if one could be performed. Barring such an analysis, the authors would be interested to discover, in practical terms, just how greatly such a program could be expanded, in terms of acquisitions and budget allocation, before it lost its performance advantages. There is also the possibility that an overly expanded program could lose its public relations advantages: if it were expanded too greatly, library patrons might eventually begin to complain that libraries had become places to order books rather than to find them. However, it does not seem from reading the current literature that the upward limit of purchase-on-demand's utility has yet been approached, and the authors are of the opinion that not only should such programs be implemented where they are lacking, but, where they are already extant, they should also be expanded.

NOTES

1. The law college's library was excluded from the study.

2. Several articles on purchase-on-demand have speculated that undergraduates purchased fewer books because they make fewer ILL requests and that science and technology patrons purchased fewer books because low program price caps and high prices disqualified their titles. This program's request records suggest an additional culprit for science and technology undergraduates: the ban on lower-level textbooks.

3. Please note that fractional discrepancies between the use values reported and the values that may be calculated using reported average prices and stock turnover rates are the result of the rounding of reported values and not of mathematical error.

4. Of the 140 LC subclasses that had had ILL acquisitions, several were eliminated for various reasons: three had only ILL acquisitions, two subclasses' traditionally acquired books had zero circulations, and the one ILL book acquired in the subclass RK also had zero circulations, so no calculations could be performed.

5. In the case of LC subclass QA, the turnover rate for an indeterminable number of traditionally acquired books had been inflated by a staff person's circulating them internally to a new books display, but ILL books in QA still had a much better use value.

6. Data for initial circulations of ILL books acquired during the first three years of the program were collected manually, and items were credited with a circulation upon receipt. Thus, there may be a small error in the early data. If later data are indicative, roughly 30 to 33 ILL-purchased books may have been credited with a false circulation.

7. Test results for the Tables 2 through 4 and Figures 5 through 7 were produced using SAS software.

REFERENCES

Allen, Megan, Suzanne M. Ward, Tanner Wray, and Karl E. Debus-López. 2003. Patron-focused services in three U.S. libraries: Collaborative interlibrary loan, collection development and acquisitions. *Interlending & Document Supply* *31*(2): 138–141.

Anderson, Kristine J., Robert S. Freeman, Jean-Pierre V. M. Herubel, Lawrence J. Mykytiuk, Judith M. Nixon, and Suzanne M. Ward. 2002. Buy, don't borrow: Bibliographers' analysis of academic library collection development through interlibrary loan requests. *Collection Management* *27*(3/4): 1–10.

Baker, Sharon L., and Karen L. Wallace. 2002. *The responsive public library: How to develop and market a winning collection.* 2nd ed. Englewood, CO: Libraries Unlimited.

Bombeld, Madeleine, and Arlene Hanerfeld. 2004. The surprising truth about faculty perception and use of collection development opportunities: One library's case study. *Against the Grain* (April): 18–22.

Bonn, George S. 1974. Evaluation of the collection. *Library Trends 22*(3): 265–304.

Brug, Sandy, and Cristi MacWaters. 2004. Patron-driven purchasing from interlibrary loan requests. *Colorado Libraries 30*(3): 36–38.

Bulick, Stephen, Wiliam N. Sabor, and Roger Flynn. 1979. Circulation and in-house use of books. In *Use of library materials: The University of Pittsburgh study*, ed. Allen Kent, Jacob Cohen, K. Leon Montgomery, James G. Williams, Stephen Bulick, Roger R. Flynn, William N. Sabor, and Una Mansfield, 9–55. New York, NY: Marcel Dekker.

Campbell, Sharon A. 2006. To buy or to borrow, that is the question. *Journal of Interlibrary Loan, Document Delivery & Electronic Reserve 16*(3): 35–39.

Chan, Gayle Rosemary Y. C. 2004. Purchase instead of borrow: An international perspective. *Journal of Interlibrary Loan, Document Delivery & Information Supply 14*(4): 23–37.

Cohen, Jacob. 1979. The economics of materials' use. In *Use of library materials: The University of Pittsburgh study*, ed. Allen Kent, Jacob Cohen, K. Leon Montgomery, James G. Williams, Stephen Bulick, Roger R. Flynn, William N. Sabor, and Una Mansfield, 105–159. New York, NY: Marcel Dekker, Inc.

Cohen, Jacob, and James R. Kern. 1979. The economics of materials' use: D. Towards a library decision model for book purchase. In *Use of library materials: The University of Pittsburgh study*, ed. Allen Kent, Jacob Cohen, K. Leon Montgomery, James G. Williams, Stephen Bulick, Roger R. Flynn, William N. Sabor, and Una Mansfield, 126–159. New York, NY: Marcel Dekker, Inc.

Comer, Alberta, and Elizabeth Lorenzen. 2006. Is purchase on demand a worthy model? Do patrons really know what they want? In *Charleston Conference Proceedings 2006*, ed. Beth R. Bernhardt, Tim Daniels, and Kim Steinle, 171–179. Charleston, SC: Libraries Unlimited.

Coopey, Barbara M., and Ann M. Snowman. 2006. ATG special report—ILL purchase express. *Against the Grain* (February): 46–49.

Davidson, John S. 1943. The use of books in a college library. *College & Research Libraries 4*(3): 294–297.

Eldredge, Jonathan D. 1998. The vital few meet the trivial many: Unexpected use patterns in a monographs collection. *Bulletin of the Medical Library Association 86*(4): 496–503.

Foss, Michelle. 2007. Books-on-demand pilot program: An innovative "patron-centric" approach to enhance the library collection. *Journal of Access Services 5*(1): 306–315.

Fussler, Herman H., and Julian L. Simon. 1969. *Patterns in the use of books in large research libraries*. Chicago: The University of Chicago Press.

Hardesty, Larry. 1981. Use of library materials at a small liberal arts college. *Library Research 3*(3): 261–282.

Houle, Louis. 2004. Convergence between interlibrary loan and acquisitions: A science and engineering library experience. Paper presented at Library Management in Changing Environment: Proceedings of the 25th annual IATUL Conference, The Library of Cracow University of Technology, Kraków, Poland, May 30—June 3, 2004. http://www.iatul.org/doclibrary/public/Conf_Proceedings/2004/Louis20Houle.pdf. Accessed July 8, 2009.

Mills, Terry R. 1982. *The University of Illinois film center collection use study*. Urbana, IL: University of Illinois, CAS Paper. (ERIC Document: ED227821).

Perdue, J., and J. Van Fleet. 1999. Borrow or buy? Cost-effective delivery of monographs. *Journal of Interlibrary Loan, Document Delivery & Information Supply* 9(4): 19–28.

Ruppel, Margie. 2006. Tying collection development's loose ends with interlibrary loan. *Collection Building* 25(3): 72–77.

Trueswell, Richard L. 1969. Some behavioral patterns of library users: The 80/20 rule. *Wilson Library Bulletin* 43(5): 458–461.

University of Nebraska-Lincoln Libraries. 2009a. Welcome. http://www.unl.edu/libr/about/. Accessed January 29, 2010.

———. 2009b. Statistics. http://www.unl.edu/libr/assessment/stats.shtml. Accessed February 5, 2010.

Vogt, W. Paul. 1999. *Dictionary of statistics and methodology: A nontechnical guide for the social science*, 2nd ed. Thousand Oaks, CA: Sage Publications, Inc.

Ward, Suzanne M. 2002. Books on demand: Just-in-time acquisitions. In *Out-of-print and special collection materials: Acquisition and purchasing options*, ed. Judith Overmier, 95–107. Simultaneously published in *The Acquisitions Librarian* 14(27): 95–107.

Ward, Suzanne M., Tanner Wray, and Karl E. Debus-López. 2003. Collection development based on patron requests: Collaboration between interlibrary loan and acquisitions. *Library Collections, Acquisitions, & Technical Services* 27(2): 203–213.

Way, Doug. 2009. The assessment of patron-initiated collection development via interlibrary loan at a comprehensive university. *Journal of Interlibrary Loan, Document Delivery & Electronic Reserve* 19(4): 299–308.

Zopfi-Jordan, David. 2008. Purchasing or borrowing: Making interlibrary loan decisions that enhance patron satisfaction. *Journal of Interlibrary Loan, Document Delivery & Electronic Reserve* 18(3): 387–394.

APPENDIX

Effective use value: As Cohen (1979) noted, data on usage become "most meaningful when combined with cost data" (105). In considering the term "effective use value" in this study, the reader should understand this to mean that the item(s) in question have a favorable (i.e., effective) ratio of cost(s) to use(s); e.g., Cohen's "total cost per item circulated ('average item cost')" or "cost per transaction ('average transaction cost')" (107–109).

Kruskal-Wallis test: This is a nonparametric test of statistical significance that is employed when testing two or more independent samples. It is a one-way analysis of variance (a type of statistical test that determines whether the means of several groups are all equal) for rank order data. (Vogt 1999, 151)

Percentage expected use (PEU): This metric is a "ratio of the percentage of use of a subject to its percentage holdings" (Mills 1982, 5) and is a modification of Bonn's use factor (see below); the modification was to multiply the use factor by 100 (7). The formula for calculating a topic's PEU is as follows: LC subclass' PEU = [(subclass' use/collection's use)/(subclass' number of items/number of items in the collection)] * 100 (to convert to a percentage).

Stock turnover rate: The rate was calculated as follows: stock turnover rate = total circulation of book X/(number of months book X was available/12).

Topical idiosyncrasy: By this expression, the authors mean that the subject of a book is of limited interest or perhaps even of interest solely to the individual who requested it.

Use factor: This term means the "ratio of use to holdings in specific subject classes" (Bonn 1974, 272) or the "[p]roportionate circulation statistics by subject class compiled over a definite period ... compared with proportionate holdings statistics by subject class" (272–273).

Use value: The average ratios were calculated as follows: use-value = Σ prices paid for all books in a category or group/ Σ annual stock turnover for all books in a category or group. This calculation should be understood to produce a ratio of prices paid to rates of annual circulation.

Own Not Loan: Different Request Sources for Purchase Lists

ERIN S. SILVA

Mathewson-IGT Knowledge Center University of Nevada, Reno, Nevada

CHERIÉ L. WEIBLE

University of Illinois at Urbana-Champaign Library, Urbana, Illinois

The interlibrary loan (ILL) department at the University of Illinois at Urbana-Champaign implemented an Own Not Loan program in 2002. The program failed due to slow turnaround time and was suspended until a better workflow could be designed. In 2008, librarians reassessed the program when the following resources became available: an acquisitions librarian who had previously worked in ILL, funding through an internal grant, and a graduate assistant trained in ILL processes. The major change between the original program and the second one was the source of the requests. In 2002, the requests were generated through the ILL department, which—unlike many other ILL operations—processes only those difficult requests that cannot be handled through I-Share, the statewide consortial borrowing program. In 2008, however, requests were generated from those requests that I-Share had been unable to fill. The article discusses the differences between the 2002 and the 2008 programs and explains how the changes made the current program successful.

OWN NOT LOAN: 2002 IMPLEMENTATION

The University of Illinois Library belongs to the Consortium of Academic and Research Libraries in Illinois (CARLI) consortium, which currently consists of over 75 libraries. In the early 2000s, librarians at the University of Illinois conducted a number of statewide studies on interlibrary loan (ILL) and collection development so that member institutions could gain better control of duplicate journal title subscriptions held within the state (Wiley and Chrzastowski 2001; Wiley and Chrzastowski 2002). Implementing the Own Not Loan patron-driven acquisitions program in the University of Illinois ILL department was a natural progression of this work.

The consortial relationship between institutions in Illinois benefits all users in the state by allowing them to draw easily on many library collections, but it is important to understand that, unlike many other academic ILL operations, the availability of I-Share means that not all user requests flow first through the ILL department. If the University of Illinois library system does not have an item, its patrons' requests for common and frequently used titles are filled through I-Share, the patron-initiated consortial borrowing system that is monitored by circulation department staff. *University of Illinois' ILL service only handles requests for titles that are not held by I-Share members*. This sound and successful practice has a number of effects on interlibrary borrowing requests. First, undergraduate students rarely need to use ILL since most of their research needs are fulfilled through the local and extended consortial collections. Second, graduate and faculty researchers are also able to obtain many of their basic research needs through these same channels. Thus, ILL generally receives only the most difficult and esoteric requests. These items are often only found in archival collections or are obtainable only through an international library or are located by extensively searching the catalogs of potential lending libraries.

When the University of Illinois at the Urbana-Champaign Library implemented the Own Not Loan program in 2002, a limited number of libraries nationwide were just beginning to use ILL requests to drive some of their purchasing and collection development practices. The Own Not Loan program started on a trial basis as a pilot program and only lasted a little over a semester. The goal was to provide materials to patrons by expediting purchases, sending them through a rush cataloging process, and adding the material to the library's collection after the patron finished using items. Parameters for purchases were simply stated: attempt to obtain materials that were unfilled through the regular ILL process. There was no initial attempt to set criteria to help inform staff about which items should be considered for the Own Not Loan program.

Unfortunately, the program was fraught with problems. The ILL and acquisitions staffs were overwhelmed, and delivery of materials was seldom timely. Other problems arose from the variety of software systems being used in ILL and acquisitions. The overall process was too time-consuming. Ultimately, users were not well-served. Librarians suspended the trial program to assess its successes and failures.

What went wrong? Fewer than a hundred items had been purchased during the pilot phase. Analysis revealed one major flaw in the initial program and showed what needed to change to implement a more successful one. Essentially, the Own Not Loan program was the right idea, but the library had chosen the wrong source for patron requests to drive the purchasing. The University of Illinois Library's ILL requests were as difficult to purchase as they were to borrow. Librarians eventually realized that the unfilled I-Share requests would provide a better source of requests for purchasing in a program like Own Not Loan.

OWN NOT LOAN: 2008 IMPLEMENTATION

The right time for the University of Illinois to start a new Own Not Loan program was January 2008. The librarian who had initiated the original Own Not Loan pilot program at Illinois now held the position of head of acquisitions and had previous experience in both ILL and circulation. An additional factor was the availability of funding in the form of an internal National Endowment for the Humanities (NEH) Challenge Grant, which provided the financial opportunity to begin a new program. The internal grant application requested $10,500; a total of $6,500 was awarded for the implementation of the new pilot program to do the following:

- Work with CARLI staff programmers to create a daily report of unfilled I-Share requests
- Fund library school graduate students to review and process the daily reports
- Fund student assistants to order, track, receive, and rush catalog material
- Fund student assistants to prepare items for patron delivery
- Fund statistics collection for program assessment

By using unfilled I-Share requests for generally mainstream titles instead of ILL requests for esoteric ones, staff hoped the new implementation would be more successful. During the new six-month pilot program, I-Share requests would drive the library's Own Not Loan purchases. After this time, the pilot would be assessed and staff would decide whether or not to add Own Not Loan as a permanent service. Success seemed even more likely because many university presses had been recently removed from the approval plan; many I-Share requests would be for titles from these publishers. Purchasing these books based on users' requests would not only fill a gap in the collection but would also better serve patrons' immediate and future research needs.

To begin the revamped process, project staff needed daily reports identifying unfilled I-Share requests and containing the following information: title, publisher, date of publication, ISBN, patron name, and patron e-mail address (which assists in ensuring that the correct person has been identified). Because users' names would be divulged, CARLI staff expressed concerns about patron privacy issues. Librarians spent some time discussing these concerns with CARLI programmers. The conversation between CARLI and the university library revolved around three points. First, CARLI already provided the library with an unfilled requests report so that the circulation department staff could find other ways to satisfy the requests. Second, only a limited number of additional library staff would see the daily report. All staff are trained and periodically reminded about patron privacy. Finally, the password-protected report could only be retrieved through a secure server. After assuring CARLI staff that patron privacy would be protected, the pilot began.

During the privacy discussions with CARLI, library staff experimented with consulting the circulation report of unfilled I-Share requests. This process proved overly complicated and was thus short-lived. At last, the graduate student who managed the Own Not Loan project was able to connect to a remote server via a Secure Shell connection to download the reports of unfilled I-Share requests several times a week. The student processed the reports in a number of ways before sending a finalized purchase request list to acquisitions. First, the text file was imported into Microsoft Excel. Erroneous or repetitive data were removed, such as multiple requests for the same title. Because only titles published in the current year or one year prior were considered for purchase, requests for older materials were removed. Because I-Share requests can be made for books held by the University of Illinois Library that are currently in use, the student checked each title in the library catalog to verify whether the item was owned or not and then recorded that information in the file. Titles already owned were not candidates for purchase. Additionally, the student maintained a master list of requests to ensure that titles were never ordered twice. After checking for and removing duplicates, the student finalized the list and sent it to acquisitions for further processing.

At this point, the acquisitions staff checked titles further to determine whether any were already on order through the approval plan or whether any were textbooks, since books would not be purchased in these cases. Then staff searched for availability through online book retailers that offer expedited shipping, such as Amazon and Barnes & Noble; items were then ordered and rush-cataloged upon receipt. The final step was to make the books available to the patrons by office delivery, if possible, or at the pickup location of their choice. Once patrons finished using the item, staff only needed to discharge the material to identify its permanent library location. Upon arrival there, the item was shelved and made available to other users for the first time.

This second implementation of the Own Not Loan program solved the main problems of the first attempt to offer a purchase-on-demand program.

By changing the source of the potential purchases to unfilled I-Share requests, books were bought, cataloged, and delivered to patrons in a timely manner. The difficult-to-obtain ILL requests were no longer used; the easier I-Share requests now drive the purchases.

CONCLUSION

After analyzing the disappointing results of the first Own Not Loan program, librarians developed a successful purchase-on-demand program. Upon realizing the different uses of ILL and I-Share and the resulting requests, librarians reconfigured Own Not Loan to transform it into a program that provided user-selected materials in a timely way. Additionally, the purchases filled gaps in the library collection. By being willing to initiate and assess the two pilot projects, the library found the best way to serve users and buy needed material for the collection.

ACKNOWLEDGEMENT

The authors would like to thank Lynn Wiley, Head of Acquisitions and Associate Professor of Library Administration, for writing the internal NEH Challenge Grant and for spearheading the work from the acquisitions department of the University of Illinois at Urbana-Champaign Library. The plan to use the failed I-Share requests to generate lists for requesting the Own Not Loan materials was entirely her idea and one that is still in practice at the time of this publication.

REFERENCES

Wiley, Lynn, and Tina E. Chrzastowski. 2001. The state of ILL in the state of IL: The Illinois Interlibrary Loan Assessment Project. *Library Collections, Acquisitions, and Technical Services* 25(1): 5–20.

Wiley, Lynn, and Tina E. Chrzastowski. 2002. The Illinois Interlibrary Loan Assessment Project II: Revisiting statewide article sharing and assessing the impact of electronic full-text journals. *Library Collections, Acquisitions, and Technical Services* 26(1): 19–33.

Just Passing Through: Patron-Initiated Collection Development in Northwest Academic Libraries

KATHLEEN CARLISLE FOUNTAIN and LINDA FREDERIKSEN

Washington State University Vancouver, Vancouver, Washington

For all academic libraries, collection development and interlibrary loan are fundamental, core activities. For a growing number of libraries, patron-initiated requests for selected materials received through interlibrary loan are passed through to acquisitions for purchase. It is unclear, however, how many of these purchase-on-demand (POD) or buy-don't-borrow programs are currently in place. The authors' research to quantify the extent of these programs in the Pacific Northwest found that POD programs are not widely used, although larger academic institutions are more likely to adopt them. Budget and workflow concerns are the major reasons for not adopting a POD program. Modeling a program after successful ones may help libraries implement a program.

INTRODUCTION

For all academic libraries, collection development and interlibrary loan are fundamental, core activities. Libraries have long been designed, built, and managed to house and circulate materials that are acquired to meet the needs of their patrons. When a library does not own an item requested by a user, interlibrary loan is commonly used as an alternative means of providing access to those items. Historically, "just-in-case" ownership and "just-in-time" access have been separate functions, both in terms of work processes and philosophy. For a growing number of libraries, however, items received as interlibrary loan requests, rather than being processed for temporary access, are instead *passed through* to acquisitions for purchase. These patron-initiated requests become part of the collection management stream in programs that are often called purchase on demand (POD) or patron-driven acquisitions. Examples of innovative and successful POD projects appear regularly in the professional literature of librarianship, providing evidence that an evolution in collection development thinking may be underway.

In North American academic libraries of all sizes and types, collection development has traditionally meant a managed system of selection, approval, and acquisition. These complex processes frequently involve bibliographers or subject specialists, recommendations from faculty, book reviews, firm orders, and approval plans. They are the means by which high-quality legacy print collections are built and managed. However, because no single library has the resources to purchase and store everything published and because monographic purchasing budgets have dramatically declined in recent years (Association for Research Libraries 2009), gaps exist in every collection. With improved discovery tools and holdings statements, the riches of the world's libraries are increasingly more findable, while unmet needs in local collections are more apparent. Each year, millions of requests for materials not available locally are routed through interlibrary loan systems and bibliographic utilities. In 2009, for example, more than ten million returnable items were borrowed and lent across the OCLC interlibrary loan system (OCLC 2009). While providing just-in-time access to library materials that help satisfy direct patron needs, resource sharing does nothing to fill permanent gaps or to build assets, equity, and use of local collections. Nor is it, in many cases, the most cost-effective or efficient means of providing material to a library's community of users (Ruppel 2006, 76). Although a completed interlibrary loan transaction does little for permanent collection building, the data the request provides can be a useful gauge of unmet needs and collection gaps. Using patron-initiated interlibrary loan requests to inform acquisition decisions is one way many libraries use data to analyze and evaluate their collections while also satisfying real patron needs.

The need for supplementary collection development models fills the literature. Many innovative *pass-through* programs and projects have been well-documented, especially during the past decade. There appears to be widespread acknowledgement that data-driven, user-centered collection development efforts and resulting POD initiatives provide numerous tangible benefits to the libraries that implement them. For an extensive literature review of this topic, see the introduction to this special issue. It is less clear, however, how many such programs are in place. It is the intention of the authors to begin to quantify the extent of POD programs while also considering prospects for expansion of what may be a new collection development model.

METHODOLOGY

The authors sought to quantify the implementation of POD programs by surveying the Pacific Northwest's academic library consortium, Orbis Cascade Alliance. The Alliance, as it is called locally, is a consortium of 36 academic libraries in Washington and Oregon. Comprising an interesting mix of large, medium, and small libraries at private and public universities, colleges, and community colleges, it serves 213,000 students (Orbis Cascade Alliance 2009). Alliance members maintain independent interlibrary loan and collection development operations, but they share a joint library catalog that facilitates unmediated patron borrowing. In addition, member libraries leverage the Alliance to purchase electronic resources at discounted rates and are currently pursuing a consortial approach to e-book purchasing. In short, member libraries support robust resource sharing across the consortium. Like all libraries, however, they reach limits of resource availability within the system.

The authors' survey consisted of 14 questions designed to collect demographic data about each library, measure the number of POD programs in place in the consortium, determine how libraries implemented their programs, and gauge the interest in POD by non-participating libraries. Using the literature describing specific POD programs around the country, the authors constructed questions that would assess the institutions' workflow. One question asked each respondent to indicate the criteria used by the library to determine whether an item was eligible to be purchased in their POD program. Two other questions allowed respondents to mark the steps they followed to purchase an item on demand. The authors targeted their survey to each main library's acquisitions or collection manager and sent that person an e-mail announcing the availability of the survey. Given that the Alliance includes a variety of academic institutions, the authors also sent surveys to collection managers in independently operating branch libraries such as law school libraries and branch campus libraries. See the Appendix for the list of institutions solicited for the survey. During the response period between January 6 and January 25, 2010, a total of 46 collection managers received the survey, and 29 completed it using SurveyMonkey.com software. The authors received notification from one respondent that her colleague answered the survey before her, so her response was removed, resulting in a remaining 28 complete surveys, for a 61% response rate.

POD PROGRAM IMPLEMENTATION

Overall, the survey results indicate that very few libraries in the consortium have implemented POD programs and, typically, those that have are large public university libraries. The authors found no factors that prove to be statistically significant indicators of whether a library will have a POD program in operation. What follows, as a result, is a snapshot of POD programs within the Orbis Cascade Alliance region.

Out of 28 libraries represented in the survey responses, only seven (25%) presently operate POD programs. Another four (14%) plan to implement a program within the next six months. Seventeen (61%), however, do not currently operate a program and have no plans to do so in the near future. Given the responses, the majority of the existing POD programs appear to be permanent components augmenting standard collection development programs. Of the seven libraries with POD programs, only three libraries have had a program in place for more than two years, while three other libraries have operated programs for longer than a year. Only one library has a new program that has yet to reach the one-year benchmark, and this pilot project is specifically funded by a gift.

Institutional Demographics

The authors were curious to see whether institutional demographics could predict whether a campus library operated a POD program. Since few libraries have POD programs in place, it was difficult to identify correlating factors. However, both institutional size and campus funding showed interesting trends. Libraries supporting student populations of 15,000 or more represented four of the seven Alliance POD programs. The remaining three programs served campuses with populations of fewer than 4,000 students. This shows an overrepresentation of programs on the large campuses and an underrepresentation of smaller campuses, given the makeup of the Alliance. Put another way, only three of 18 small-campus libraries had programs, although four of six large-campus libraries had POD programs (see Figure 1).

Equally noticeable is the overrepresentation of publicly funded academic libraries operating POD programs. Public institutions represented 44% of the responses but 71% of the programs. Privately funded libraries, in contrast, provided 56% of the survey responses but have only 29% of the Alliance's POD programs.

Program Implementation

With this survey, the authors wished to uncover implementation trends for POD programs that could guide other libraries considering this endeavor. Questions about process, budget, and vendors reveal striking similarities across institutions. Most libraries fulfill their requests through Amazon, but do not necessarily rely on Amazon alone to satisfy all acquisitions needs. Respondents could choose all of the vendors turned to for POD requests,

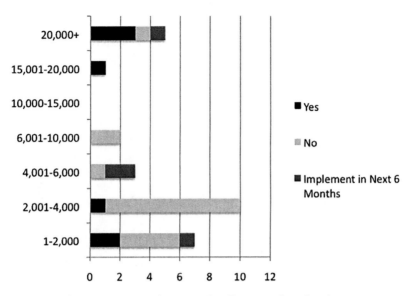

FIGURE 1 Size of institutions in Orbis Cascade Alliance with and without POD programs.

and many reported using Amazon in combination with Alibris (at times billed through OCLC) or YBP. Others mentioned that they used Baker & Taylor as well as foreign vendors (see Table 1).

One of the most significant roadblocks for those libraries yet to experiment with POD is funding. Six of the respondents with existing programs offer guidance on how to designate funds: three libraries tap into their general book budget; two created a specific POD allocation; and one library designated gift funds for the express purpose of testing its program. None of these libraries relied on specific subject allocations or passed along costs to individual subject selectors.

To keep costs under control, libraries typically apply a list of criteria to requested books before placing orders. Again, trends emerged for libraries currently operating programs and those that are in the planning stages. One criterion appears to be universally important to all libraries with current programs: "appropriateness to the collection" (see Table 2).

TABLE 1 Purchase on Demand Vendors

Vendor	No.	% of Respondents
Amazon	6	85.7%
Alibris	4	57.1%
Other	4	57.1%
YBP	3	42.9%
Total respondents	8	

Respondents could select all vendors that applied. Percentages add up to more than 100%.

TABLE 2 Criteria for Purchasing Interlibrary Loan Requests

Criteria	Existing Programs	Planned Programs
Appropriateness to the collection	6	3
Unavailable for borrowing locally through summit	4	3
Request received from an eligible borrower	4	3
Falls under specified cost limit	4	2
Unavailable for borrowing through interlibrary loan	3	1
Recent publication date: less than 1–2 years old	2	2
Rush purchase available from supplier	2	2
Other	1	0
Total respondents	6	4

Respondents could select all criteria that applied.

Some librarians commented on additional criteria. One library previously limited requests to books but recently expanded eligibility to include DVDs and music scores. Another reported looking at the patron's time frame to determine whether a purchased item could satisfy the request in time. Budget factors influenced the process for two libraries. In one case, the "availability of funds" could restrict the use of POD. Another library described using a $35 per-item cost limit, but does not automatically process the interlibrary loan request as a purchase unless it is the second time the item has been requested.

To better understand how items move from request to fulfillment, the authors provided a list of steps and asked respondents to select the steps used in order of procedures (see Table 3). All processes started with a request received through interlibrary loan, and six libraries have the interlibrary loan staff automatically examine the request against their POD criteria to

TABLE 3 Step-by-Step Workflow, from Request Received to Item Ordered

Action	Step 1	Step 2	Step 3	Step 4	Step 5
Request received in interlibrary loan for an unowned item	7	0	0	0	0
Interlibrary loan staff examine item against POD criteria	0	6	0	0	0
Request routed to acquisitions/collections for decision making	0	0	2	0	0
Request routed to acquisitions/collections to order	0	0	3	2	0
Request placed immediately into fulfillment software	0	0	1	0	1
Request routed to subject liaison for review and purchase decision	0	1	1	0	0
Total respondents	7	7	7	2	1

determine eligibility for purchase. From there, the process varies from library to library. Four of seven libraries proceed directly to ordering the item. Another three libraries send the request to either the acquisitions/collections department or to a subject specialist for a purchase decision; then the item is ordered.

Clarifying comments from librarians helped to provide a realistic sense of how POD programs operate in different libraries. One librarian noted that the library does not use the program extensively, but discussions take place to determine whether the book will be added to the collection. If so, the ordering process begins. Another librarian shared that the library had previously rushed all POD orders from vendors, but changed procedures in response to "the patron's need date." As a result, order titles were rushed less frequently, which saves money.

The process from receiving the ordered item to ultimately shelving it in the stacks proved to be nearly identical in each library (see Table 4). There are only two notable differences among the seven libraries. The first is whether full or minimal book processing happens in advance of circulation to the patron. Six of eight respondents conduct full processing when the item arrives. The second difference is whether the item is immediately added to the collection or reviewed for permanent inclusion. Five of seven libraries automatically add the item to the collection and shelve it in the stacks, while the two that conduct only minimal processing do so because they will later evaluate its suitability to the collection. One respondent selected both

TABLE 4 Step-by-Step Workflow, from Item Received to Shelving in Stack

Action	Step 1	Step 2	Step 3	Step 4	Step 5	Step 6	Step 7	Step 8
Purchase received	7	0	0	0	0	0	0	0
Minimal processing for circulation	0	2	0	0	0	0	0	0
Full processing rushed for circulation	0	6	0	0	0	0	0	0
Patron notified that the item is available	0	0	7	0	0	0	0	0
Item checked out to patron	0	0	0	7	0	0	0	0
Patron returns the item	0	0	0	0	7	0	0	0
Decision made to keep item in permanent collection	0	0	0	0	0	2	0	0
Item is routed to technical services for full processing	0	0	0	0	0	0	2	0
Item is shelved in the stacks	0	0	0	0	0	5	0	2
Total respondents	7	8*	7	7	7	7	2	2

*One respondent selected both full and minimal processing in the same step because processing depended on the needs of the patron.

full and minimal processing in the same step and added a comment that processing depended on the needs of the patron and how quickly he or she needed the item.

POD AS A NEW COLLECTION DEVELOPMENT MODEL

Patron-initiated collection development does not begin and end with POD programs. The profession has been examining the next wave of demand-based acquisitions, patron-initiated e-book purchasing (Nelson 2000; Price and McDonald 2009). The Orbis Cascade Alliance librarians were asked whether they wished to adapt their POD programs to incorporate e-books. Surprisingly, only four libraries are interested in a patron-initiated e-book–purchasing program, while six either are not now interested or do not know whether they will move to such a program (see Table 5).

More interestingly, the comments shed light on why there are so few plans to move to patron-initiated e-book purchasing. Two respondents would like to do so, but structural impediments prevent effective implementation. One librarian noted that it is not possible to loan e-books to consortial partners, which is a "very big issue for us." Another remarked that POD for e-books would not be possible with current models because "it is not possible with WorldCat Local," the platform for the consortium's joint library catalog.

In the Orbis Cascade Alliance, most of the libraries are not operating POD programs. Since much of the published literature on POD programs focused on large research libraries and the Alliance comprises a high percentage of small institutions, the authors anticipated this response. One survey question asked librarians to select and comment on the most significant barriers to implementing a POD program. Two factors proved the most problematic for libraries: (1) budget and (2) staffing and workflow (see Table 6).

The comments provide a more nuanced picture of institutional barriers. For example, staffing and workflow are significant impediments at one institution where faculty members serve as primary book selectors for the library. The assumption one can make from this is that no separate budget exists to purchase monographs, and staffing is set up to respond to faculty selections rather than to any other purchase requests. Another librarian viewed POD as a threat to resource sharing, and the library wanted to support the

TABLE 5 Plan to Adapt Purchase on Demand to Include e-Books

	Existing Programs	Planned Programs
Yes	2	2
No	1	1
Don't know	3	1
Total	6	4

TABLE 6 Greatest Barrier to Implementing Purchase on Demand Programs

Barrier	No.	% of Responses
Budget	8	42.1%
Staffing and workflow	8	42.1%
Other	3	15.8%
Administrative support	0	0.0%
Size of library	0	0.0%
Total	19	100%

consortium by keeping requests within the interlibrary loan system. Some libraries simply have not undertaken this effort due to institutional inertia and rely instead on long-established collection development and resource-sharing practices.

LESSONS LEARNED FROM THE ORBIS CASCADE ALLIANCE

Although the survey results do not present a statistically significant indication that POD programs are, as yet, widely used in the region, a number of interesting factors emerged: POD programs are generally more widely adopted by large institutions; the programs in existence follow comparable workflows, although there is not one standardized model; and, finally, Alliance libraries have similar reasons for not adopting POD programs. Nearly half of the libraries without POD programs cite their budget as a primary factor prohibiting implementation. The Alliance can offer guidance to these libraries. For those wishing to keep costs under control, a limited allocation would allow libraries to test a system that could be discontinued when the allocation is spent. A predefined list of criteria for POD purchases would help protect the budget and simplify the ordering workflow. From this study, it is clear that there are several standard criteria used to limit the volume of purchases. A library staff member could begin by defining limits using the most straightforward criteria identified in the survey:

- The item is unavailable from local consortial lenders.
- An eligible borrower sent in the request, such as faculty and graduate student requestors only.
- The purchase cost falls under a specified limit, such as the estimated average interlibrary loan cost.
- The item has a very recent publication date, such as published in the last year.

Once these parameters are established, the staff can determine whether they want to limit purchases to those appropriate to the collection, which would involve a more complicated discussion on how to determine "appropriateness." These criteria would be the simplification of the workflow and provide front-line staff with clear directions for determining what items should be sent forward for further evaluation or purchase.

Finally, this study found clear trends in POD workflows. Libraries planning to implement POD programs can adopt the Alliance workflow, test it with their pilot project, and modify it as needed. The following emerged as the typical model:

1. Request received through interlibrary loan channels.
2. Interlibrary loan staff members compare the request to the POD criteria.
3. Order placed by interlibrary loan or acquisitions staff OR request immediate review by a librarian, then ordered.
4. Item received.
5. Full processing performed.
6. Patron notified that item is ready for checkout.
7. Patron checks out then returns item.
8. Item shelved in stacks.

Concerns of Alliance libraries are typical of universities across the country, and it is clear that planning for POD programs must involve consideration of budget concerns, program guidelines, and staff workflows. Overwhelmingly, however, the respondents to this survey see the value of using data derived from patron-initiated interlibrary loan requests to inform and supplement book acquisition decisions. This survey shows that large campus libraries in the Orbis Cascade Alliance have embraced POD programs as part of their collection development operations. Smaller campus libraries, however, have not widely adopted such programs despite recognizing their potential value. The authors hope that the models discussed in this article enable more libraries to implement their own patron-driven purchasing programs.

ACKNOWLEDGEMENT

The authors wish to thank Rich Alldredge, Ph.D., of the Washington State University Department of Statistics for his assistance with the statistical analysis.

REFERENCES

Association of Research Libraries. 2009. *ARL Statistics 2007–2008*. http://www.arl. org/bm˜doc/arlstat08.pdf (accessed February 12, 2010).

Nelson, Barbara K. 2000. Conference report: Future of e-books in the role of scholarly communication and distance. *Library Collections, Acquisitions, & Technical Services 24*: 416–420.

OCLC. 2009. *OCLC Annual Report, 2008/2009.* http://www.oclc.org/news/publications/annualreports/2009/2009.pdf (accessed May 24, 2010).

Orbis Cascade Alliance. 2009. *Orbis Cascade Alliance.* http://www.orbiscascade.org/ (accessed May 24, 2010).

Price, Jason, and John McDonald. 2009. Beguiled by bananas: A retrospective study of the usage and breadth of patron vs. librarian acquired e-book collections. Presented at the annual Charleston Conference, Charleston, SC, November 5, http://www.katina.info/conference/2009presentations/Thurs2_Price.pdf (accessed May 24, 2010).

Ruppel, Margie. 2006. Tying collection development's loose ends with interlibrary loan. *Collection Building* 25(3): 72–77.

APPENDIX

Orbis Cascade Alliance Libraries, 2010

Central Oregon Community College
Bend, Oregon
Central Washington University
Ellensburg, Washington
Chemeketa Community College
Salem, Oregon
Clark College
Vancouver, Washington
Concordia University
Portland, Oregon
Eastern Oregon University
LaGrande, Oregon
Eastern Washington University
Cheney, Washington
George Fox University
Newberg, Oregon
Lane Community College
Eugene, Oregon
Lewis & Clark College
Portland, Oregon
Linfield College
McMinnville, Oregon
Marylhurst University
Portland, Oregon
Mt. Hood Community College
Gresham, Oregon
Oregon Health & Science University/
    Portland, Oregon
Oregon Institute of Technology
Klamath Falls, Oregon
Oregon State University
Corvallis, Oregon
Pacific University
Forest Grove, Oregon
Portland Community College
Portland, Oregon

Portland State University
Portland, Oregon
Reed College
Portland, Oregon
Saint Martin's University
Lacey, Washington
Seattle Pacific University
Seattle, Washington
Seattle University
Seattle, Washington
Southern Oregon University
Ashland, Oregon
The Evergreen State College
Olympia, Washington
University of Oregon
Eugene, Oregon
University of Portland
Portland, Oregon
University of Puget Sound
Tacoma, Washington
University of Washington
Seattle, Washington
Walla Walla University
Walla Walla. Washington
Warner Pacific College
Portland, Oregon
Washington State
    University
Pullman, Washington
Western Oregon University
Monmouth, Oregon
Western Washington University
Bellingham, Washington
Whitman College
Walla Walla, Washington
Willamette University
Salem, Oregon

Resolving the Challenge of E-Books

DRACINE HODGES, CYNDI PRESTON, and MARSHA J. HAMILTON

The Ohio State University, Columbus, Ohio

The authors identify the major issues associated with e-books and their expanding role in libraries, especially in patron-driven acquisitions. E-book access began when NetLibrary entered the patron-driven acquisitions arena in the late 1990s with a business model that raised concerns for some libraries and their patrons. Since then, other models and variations abound. Today the library community would prefer far greater uniformity across e-book publishers in areas such as simultaneous publishing, printing ability, access models, resource sharing use, and compatibility with handheld reading devices, among others. Libraries would acquire even more e-books, providing even more revenue for publishers, if these issues could be resolved.

Many libraries first experimented with acquiring e-books in the 1990s, following the Project Gutenberg example, when they digitized historic treasures from their own collections, including rare books, manuscripts, photographs, and sound recordings. Examples include the British Library's digitization of the only known manuscript of the epic poem *Beowulf* and the Library of Congress' *American Memory* project, a substantial digitized collection of American historical documents and media (Lebert 2009, chap. 1998). At about the same time, publishers began offering individual e-book titles for sale, including more recent imprints. The paradigm shift to patron-initiated e-book collection development occurred in 1998 when NetLibrary offered libraries three acquisitions methods: orders for individual titles or subject packages of e-books; a notification service for librarian selection; and the patron-driven acquisition model. The patron-driven acquisitions model allowed patrons to act as de facto collection development personnel. Patron use of e-books triggered purchases, bypassing mediation by a collection development librarian.

The original NetLibrary business model raised concerns for some libraries. A purchase was triggered after an e-book was accessed for the second time; the second view could consist of as little as viewing a single page, the equivalent of a patron browsing a print book and returning it to the shelf without checking it out. Some libraries were not willing to finance this level of e-book browsing. NetLibrary also adopted the model of a circulation period. The library established a check-out period, such as two weeks, during which the e-book was available only to the patron who had "borrowed" it. The book would only be available to others when the check-out period expired or the borrower went through a nonintuitive process to "return" the e-book. NetLibrary printing was limited to one page at a time to discourage copyright violation, a limitation that many patrons found highly restrictive. Patrons also disliked the need to create a NetLibrary account after authenticating in the local system or via IP address.

Some libraries participated in a NetLibrary patron-driven acquisitions program through a consortium. For example, The Ohio State University Libraries (OSUL) used its OhioLINK membership to allow patrons to access NetLibrary titles. NetLibrary's business model quickly triggered more purchases than anticipated, so OSUL blocked patron purchase of additional titles. OhioLINK experimented with several short periods of NetLibrary patron-driven acquisitions but discontinued adding titles after 2004. NetLibrary was purchased by OCLC in 2002, becoming OCLC NetLibrary. It changed hands again in 2010 when it was acquired by EBSCO.

Complications in creating a sustainable business model delayed expansion of patron-initiated acquisitions programs in the 2000s. Worried that e-books would cut into hardcover sales, publishers searched for a model that would protect revenue streams. As aggregators, they depended on profit to stay in business and to develop new products, while libraries dealt with skyrocketing costs for e-journals and databases in a period of stable or shrinking budgets.

Pricing models were not the only concern. Availability was also an issue. Some publishers, like ABC-CLIO, adopted simultaneous publication for print and e-content, a move much appreciated by libraries, while other publishers embargoed e-books for three to 18 months after publication to protect print sales. Even when an e-book was made available for purchase, some publishers imposed an additional delay before e-books could be included in leased collections. Lack of uniformity across the publishing industry causes ongoing problems for aggregators and libraries alike. OCLC NetLibrary's attempt to adapt to nonstandard publishing practices could be seen in its purchase threshold being set at one, two, or three accesses depending on the publisher. Trying to explain to patrons these access and printing limitations across multiple e-book platforms continues to be a challenge for public service librarians. Libraries will be watching to see whether EBSCO Publishing responds to the demands of the growing e-book marketplace. Negotiating with publishers for the simultaneous release of titles in both print and e-book formats would be a good place to start.

As e-books rise in popularity, the case for simultaneous publication with print formats gains importance. Acquisitions librarians may be reminded of similar delayed publication controversies in the past for hardcover versus paperback editions and U.K. vs. U.S. editions. The same issues appear in the current print versus e-book simultaneous publication discussion. The supply of U.K. versus U.S. editions has been addressed by several vendor-based services such as Blackwell's Preferred Edition Service, in which libraries can impose price and release date parameters to their U.S. or U.K. approval profiles. Expanding on this model, some vendors and e-book aggregators like YBP market integrated e-book and print approval profiles so libraries can avoid duplication between formats or get e-books as the preferred format for titles with simultaneous publication. However, until simultaneous publication becomes common practice, preferred format services will have limited success.

Many publishers' current business models rely heavily on revenue generated by print sales; some are reluctant to adapt to the evolving e-book marketplace. According to that business model, the longer the hardcover edition is the sole source of content, the more money the publisher makes. After hardcover sales peak, a paperback edition often has its run. At some point the publisher releases the e-book, first for sale, and later by permission to include the e-book in leased collections. The timing of each release is based on a schedule that publishers hope will maximize profit. In the e-book versus print debate, this model becomes irrelevant because there is no cost differential between hardcover and e-book editions. The majority of e-books sell at the hardcover list price or higher, sometimes substantially higher, for multiple user options. Few libraries want to buy both the hardcover and the e-book; they cannot afford to buy the same content twice. So, should the library defer buying the title while only the hardcover is available in the hope that the e-book will be released soon? Or buy the hardcover and forgo eventual purchase of the e-book, a format that many patrons now prefer?

Academic research librarians are discussing e-book–preferred policies for several reasons. First is the changing demographic of users, who increasingly expect to interact virtually with information and desire the convenience of remote 24/7 access. Many libraries also are faced with space and storage issues and their related costs. The cost of monographs in science, technology, and medicine climbed substantially in the 2000s. Leasing e-book packages or consortial purchasing of e-books helps address these factors. However, without simultaneous publication, libraries may not buy new print titles at all while they wait for the embargo to expire for the preferred e-book format.

In this new environment, publishers run the risk that while waiting for the e-book release, a library may decide not to purchase their title at all.

The irony in the campaign for simultaneous e-book publication is that most publishers, including some smaller presses, have adopted digital publishing for the production and/or distribution of their print and electronic content. The transformation of the commercial marketplace has encouraged a growing number of publishers to adopt the epub standard, a digital file extension of an XML format for reflowable digital books and publications. Reflowable content can be sent to various display devices without the need for reformatting. According to the International Digital Publishing Forum Web site, a trade and standards association for the digital publishing industry, "This flexibility allows publishers to produce and send a single digital publication file through to distribution and offers consumers interoperability between software and hardware for unencrypted reflowable digital books and other publications" (International). This type of platform allows transfer of e-content to devices with e-reader applications, like the Amazon Kindle and Sony Reader, and smart phones such as the Apple iPhone. Dropping e-content embargoes and using the epub standard for delivery would create adaptable content for users who increasingly expect electronic access to new titles.

Some publishers have instituted retrodigitization projects to mine their backlist titles. There have been cases where noncirculating print titles have gained a second life as e-books. In addition to providing 24/7 access, e-books provide full-text searching. The discovery possibilities of e-books can, in turn, generate increased circulation for some print titles among readers who may identify content in the e-book but prefer to use the library's print copy to read longer texts or for long-term research. This is an example of the e-book's value as a gateway to existing print editions.

Numerous smaller presses have begun using digital publishing for the print-on-demand or publish-on-demand model in which copies of a book are not printed until an order is received. Providing the title in e-book format when it is originally published creates the opportunity to mirror this model in a patron-initiated environment through *use on demand*. Use takes the place of a traditional order when the patron interacts sufficiently with the e-book to trigger its purchase.

One still unresolved issue is that although chapters can usually be provided from e-books in fulfillment of an interlibrary loan requests, entire e-books cannot be lent. Libraries may also face restrictions if they wish to use e-books as course reserves. Finally, e-book aggregators' current patron-driven acquisitions models and features are sufficiently different that it can be very difficult to compare them and choose the best option for a library's patrons.

Publishers' reluctance to experiment with new revenue streams and the budgetary crises in libraries remain intractable problems for expanding the choices and availability of e-books in libraries, especially through patron-initiated acquisition initiatives. However, format flexibility and adapting to the evolving needs and expectations of library customers and their patrons may finally provide the tipping point in the balance between simultaneous publication of print and e-books. Today is a time of transition; libraries, publishers, and vendors are experimenting with a variety of options. This special issue presents many ideas in the evolving area of patron-driven acquisitions and brings us one step closer to resolving the challenge of including e-books in that effort.

REFERENCES

International Digital Publishing Forum. Available at: http://www.openebook.org/specs.htm (accessed March 9, 2010).

Lebert, Marie. 2009. *A short history of e-books.* Project Gutenberg. http://www.gutenberg.org/etext/29801 (accessed May 24, 2010).

Developing a Multiformat Demand-Driven Acquisition Model

MICHAEL LEVINE-CLARK

University of Denver, Denver, Colorado

This paper discusses a patron-driven acquisition program at the University of Denver. Instead of selecting books from YBP's slip approval plan, the Penrose Library will load MARC records for these titles and for a selection of electronic books from ebrary and EBL. All University of Denver students and faculty will be able to select the title and format (print or electronic) that best suits their needs, thereby allowing the library to expend its collection funds in a more user-oriented way. Through this demand-driven acquisition model, the library offers its users a much wider range of titles, while ensuring that more of the titles purchased are used.

INTRODUCTION

Academic libraries have traditionally purchased books based on an assessment of quality and suitability for local research and curricular needs. Books were, and still are, bought largely for the potential that they might someday be used. This model has always made sense: books must be available at the point of need, books have to be purchased before they go out of print, and books should be set on the library's shelves to allow for serendipitous discovery. But scholarly publishing is changing in ways that make it possible to rethink how, and when, libraries buy books. As academic publishers and libraries make the transition to e-books, books will no longer go out of print; libraries will be able to purchase e-books at the point of need instead of at the time of publication. And the range of bibliographic tools available to users, such as WorldCat, makes it far less important that books can be browsed on the shelf.

The University of Denver's Penrose Library has been working with Blackwell Book Services, which is now owned by YBP, to develop a demand-driven acquisition plan for paper and digital monographs. This plan will allow users access to a much larger universe of titles in the catalog than was ever possible under the traditional just-in-case model, and it will allow them to make decisions about which format of a title suits their information needs.

WHY DEMAND-DRIVEN ACQUISITION?

As at most academic libraries, a large percentage of books at the University of Denver do not get used and probably never will be used (Lugg et al. 2010). Of the 89,496 titles published between 2005 and 2009 in the University of Denver collections, 47,257 (53%) have not circulated; 21,810 (24%) have circulated only once; and 20,429 (23%) have circulated two or more times. Use patterns will improve over time, but a comparison with books that have been in the collection since 2005 indicates that the circulation rate does not increase by much: limiting to books with a 2005 imprint date, 9,112 titles (42%) have not circulated; 5,258 (25%) have circulated once; and 7,124 (33%) have circulated two or more times. If 40% or more of books never circulate and 25% circulate only once, librarians need to reconsider which books are purchased.

While many of the books that the University of Denver purchased have very low use, the university has only been able to buy a very small percentage of the books published annually. In a typical year, Penrose Library purchases between 20,000 and 25,000 books. Yet in 2008, 170,663 books of all types, scholarly and popular, were published in North America (Barr and Harbison 2009). In fiscal year 2008, Blackwell treated 53,869 books on approval in North America. This number is a good approximation of the scholarly monographic output for that year. In the same fiscal year, Penrose Library received 23,097 slip notifications from Blackwell and ordered 9,800 titles (42%) from those slips.

Rather than purchasing a small portion of the scholarly books published in a given year only to see them sit on the shelf unused, the librarians at the University of Denver decided to make the titles announced by Blackwell on slips available for users to discover by loading MARC records into the catalog. Once the decision was made to add all Blackwell titles from the slip approval plan to the catalog, the library also decided to expand the program to include e-books from EBL and ebrary. The library had been part of the original NetLibrary demand-driven consortial model in the late 1990s and has since subscribed to some e-book packages and purchased a few others, but it has done almost no purchasing of e-books on a title-by-title basis since about 2003. This change would provide users with immediate access to books, something the library felt was crucial as it moved into the demand-driven model.

THE MODEL

Penrose Library has had an approval plan with Blackwell for many years and has received about 7,500 books annually. In the demand-driven model, the book approval plan will continue unchanged. However, since Blackwell has merged with YBP, librarians will work with YBP on reprofiling to make the new plan as similar to the old one as possible. This plan will continue to include automatic delivery of some books, because many users need books right away and cannot or will not wait for a book to be delivered. In the future, e-books will almost certainly meet the need for instant access, but currently there are not enough scholarly monographs available in e-versions to meet that need. YBP estimates that approximately 20% of the books that are covered in a given year are available in both electronic and print formats.

The major change that the demand-driven model will make in the approval plan will be in the slip notification service. Penrose Library normally bought over 9,000 books a year from slip notifications. Instead of buying these up front, the library will load MARC records for these books into the catalog, giving users the option to request a purchase. Some types of books, most notably reprints, will still need librarian mediation, although these may be inspected simply to see whether the original edition is already owned before being loaded into the catalog for potential purchase. Titles in the slip notification section of the profile are the logical area to begin a demand-driven acquisition program for print monographs because the library has already identified interest in these subjects. The fact that these titles show up on slips rather than as automatically delivered books means either that they are lower-priority or that too much is published in a given year for the library to buy all titles on that subject automatically. In either case, this change will give users a larger list of books and allow them to select these titles based on their own needs. When users discover the MARC record for the print version of a book in the library's catalog, they will be able to click on a link stating "request a purchase of this book." This will bring them to a Web page that explains that the book, although not currently owned by the library, will be purchased for them. The page includes information on how long it will take to get the book and whether an e-version is available. Users will then be able to fill out a purchase request form.

E-books will also be included in the demand-driven acquisition plan. Because selection of e-books can trigger an immediate and seamless purchase, unnoticed by the user, e-books are the perfect medium for demand-driven acquisition. The library is working with EBL to identify a universe of appropriate titles to allow users a wide choice of e-books, and it will be expanding the project to include another e-book vendor in the near future. Because e-book vendors have different pools of titles available, different platforms, and different models for demand-driven acquisition, it seems worthwhile to work with multiple vendors during the initial phase of the project. This wide choice will allow users to select the platform they prefer and allow the library to experiment with different models of demand-driven e-book acquisition and gather data on which model users prefer. EBL has a sophisticated model for demand-driven acquisition. Depending on library preferences, the first n uses can be rentals, and those rentals can be set to different lengths and costs by different libraries. Because of the relatively low number of books with four or more circulations, the University of Denver is using a model wherein a purchase is not triggered until after the third rental. The first three times a user accesses the book for more than five minutes (a free browsing period) are rentals. The library does not purchase the book until the fourth use. Models from other e-book vendors do not yet involve rentals; instead, a purchase occurs after multiple free uses. University of Denver librarians prefer a model like EBL's that involves rentals followed by purchase, and they have been discussing this with other vendors.

MARC records from EBL and the other e-book vendor(s) will be loaded into the catalog. Users who discover those e-books will then click on the URL in the record, get a description of the book in the vendor's system, and decide whether to click into the e-book. Once a version of the e-book has been purchased (not rented), the other vendor's version will be blocked from purchase and the MARC record will be removed from the catalog. Although this is not an ideal system, the library and YBP plan to develop a model that works more efficiently for other libraries during this pilot project.

Users will also be able to discover e-books directly from within the e-book vendors' databases. The library has had discussions with several vendors about the possibility of providing a link from the vendor database record to the MARC record in the library's catalog for the print version of the books. Though not possible yet, this would allow users greater choice in determining which format, paper or electronic, they prefer.

Penrose Library has decided to allow duplication between print and electronic versions of the book, as long as that duplication is intentional. In many cases a user will prefer the e-book because it can be accessed immediately or away from the library and because it can be searched. In other cases, users may prefer a print copy because of a preference for paper or a desire for more immersive reading. Since the point of demand-driven acquisition is to respond directly to user needs and preferences, allowing a format and platform choice is desirable. Once an e-book has been selected, the user will have immediate access. This use will generate a rental or purchase, which will in turn lead to that title appearing on a monthly invoice. Once e-books have been purchased, ownership will be noted in the record and alternate versions of that e-book will be removed from the catalog. Users will have immediate access and will not be aware that their use has sparked a purchase.

Selection of a print book is more complicated, and some details still need to be worked out. Requests for purchase of print monographs will be queued for processing by the acquisitions department. The acquisitions department will examine this list daily; books below $125 will be ordered immediately, while books over that price will require mediation by a selector. Orders will be sent to YBP to be fulfilled on an expedited basis. Those orders may be shipped directly to the end user, with a signature upon receipt allowing YBP to pass a check-out time on to the library. Ultimately, this entire process needs to be automated, but for now it will require some staff intervention.

CONCERNS

Although University of Denver librarians think that users will welcome demand-driven acquisition of monographs, there are several factors that could cause some aspects of the project to fail. There is a question about how users will react to the presence in the catalog of records for unowned print monographs. Users may find it confusing and frustrating to discover a book in the catalog that they cannot access immediately. On the other hand, users may be pleased to discover many more books through the catalog than was possible in the past. A second concern is one of fiscal uncertainty. The library will be loading many more records into the catalog than it can ever afford. The expectation, of course, is that users will only request a subset of the titles represented by those records. But if use of the new service is significantly higher than use of the current collection, the library would spend its funds faster than planned. Although this would be a problem, there is a fairly easy solution: once funds have been expended, MARC records will be suppressed and e-books will be blocked from vendor databases until the start of the new fiscal year. A third concern is that the library will end up spending the same amount of money as it did in the past on fewer monographs. It might buy many duplicate print and electronic versions of the same titles and might spend more money on first renting and then purchasing some e-books than it would have on simply buying them in the first place. If users choose both electronic and print formats, and if use justifies that duplication, then that may be considered a better use of funds than purchasing a wider range of unused titles. If there are patterns in particular areas of high print/electronic duplication, the library may be able to negotiate a discount for a bundled purchase from the publisher. And if the library notices patterns of high rental before purchase, it may be able to use those statistics to identify subjects to purchase upfront. A fourth concern, the major worry, is the following question: if libraries move en masse to a demand-driven acquisition model, what will be the impact on scholarly publishing? Can monographs on narrow subjects still be published if no library will purchase them at the time of publication? What might be the impact on publishing, on tenure and promotion, and on scholarship in general, especially in the humanities?

ASSESSMENT

As the library makes the transition to a demand-driven acquisition model for scholarly monographs, it will be crucial to assess patrons' reactions. The library plans to do this in a number of ways. First, users will have the choice to fill out a feedback form when presented with the option of requesting purchase of a print book. They will also be sent a form when a requested print book is delivered. Combined, these feedback mechanisms should provide input about users' opinions of demand-driven acquisition of printed books. The library conducted a major survey about the use of e-books in the university community in 2005 (Levine-Clark 2006; Levine-Clark 2007) and again in the spring of 2010. The results indicate that for many users and for many uses, e-books are acceptable or even preferable. The survey will be repeated again after the demand-driven model has been in place.

The library will also gather data from librarians. Selectors in the participating subject areas will go through the motions of "ordering" books from approval plan slips throughout the first year of the project. This activity will allow comparison of what selectors would have ordered with what users ultimately did order. It will help to determine any potential savings, any areas where the approval plan may be adjusted, and any other changes that might be needed to improve the demand-driven acquisition process.

Finally, the library will look closely at the use data for the print and electronic books purchased through this project. Depending on usage, titles in some subjects could be purchased automatically on approval, while those in other subjects might be blocked entirely. Usage might indicate user preferences for a particular e-book platform, for e-books in some subjects and print books in others, or for different treatments, depending on the publisher.

CONCLUSIONS

It is anticipated that the University of Denver's transition to demand-driven acquisition of scholarly monographs will allow purchase of a better selection of books for its users than it has in the past. Instead of buying 20,000 books each year and watching 40% go unused, the library will purchase books that users select. Librarians anticipate that this will mean higher use for those titles. Furthermore, the demand-driven acquisition plan will allow selectors to spend more time on harder-to-find material. Ultimately, it should provide users a better mix of monographs than they have had in the past.

The ideal demand-driven acquisition model would make all books currently covered by the approval plan available as both print and e-books; users would immediately get the books that they need in the format they want. But the publishing industry is not ready for that model. Only a small portion of titles published in a given year is available as e-books, and an even smaller portion is available at or near the time of publication of the print book. Until this situation changes within the publishing industry, the University of Denver will experiment with the model described above.

REFERENCES

Barr, Catherine, and Constance Harbison. 2009. Book title output and average prices: 2004–2008. In *Library and Book Trade Almanac 2009*, 504–512. Medford, NJ: Information Today, Inc.

Levine-Clark, M. 2006. Electronic Book Usage. *portal: Libraries and the Academy 6*: 285–299.

———. 2007. Electronic books and the humanities: A survey at the University of Denver. *Collection Building 26*(1): 7–14.

Lugg, Rick, Cory Tucker, and Chris Sugnet. 2010. Library collaboration and the changing environment: An interview with Rick Lugg, R2 Consulting. *Collaborative Librarianship 2*(1): 19–21.

Patron-Initiated Collection Development: Progress of a Paradigm Shift

DRACINE HODGES, CYNDI PRESTON, and MARSHA J. HAMILTON

The Ohio State University, Columbus, Ohio

This article discusses a paradigm shift from librarian-mediated collection development to patron-initiated selection of library materials. The authors report on two programs at The Ohio State University Libraries (OSUL): an interlibrary loan purchase-on-demand program and two tests of ebrary's patron-driven acquisitions program, in which patron usage triggered behind-the-scenes purchase of e-books. Results of the tests were analyzed by user activity, subject area, publisher type and level, and imprint date. OSUL and OhioLINK consortium holdings were reviewed to evaluate availability, duplication, and circulation of titles purchased by patrons. OSUL subject librarians were polled for comments on patron-selected titles and the funding implications of patron-driven selection. The authors discuss changes in the philosophy of collection development, and the role of patrons and collection development librarians in the evolving e-book environment in academic libraries.

FROM LIBRARIAN SELECTION TO LIBRARIAN-MEDIATED PATRON SELECTION

Academic libraries have traditionally allowed patron input on purchasing decisions, from the suggestion box to online request forms, but the authority for collection development ultimately resided with librarians. Technology and economic factors have positioned a paradigm to shift. This article examines the progression from librarian-mediated to patron-initiated collection development and the factors driving it. The shift will be illustrated with programs at the Ohio State University Libraries (OSUL).

During the expansion of Ohio State University following World War II, with classrooms overflowing with GI Bill students, library acquisitions funds increased along with the number of subject specialists hired to build the collections. The postwar ideal was to build a research library to meet the needs of existing and future patrons. This was the "just-in-case" model of collection development. It was the bibliographer's job to identify the best materials, and the job of the acquisitions department to acquire them. Items requested by patrons could be ordered, but the bibliographer strove to anticipate the needs of faculty and students, by being familiar with their research and classes, and to purchase titles in advance of need.

As decades passed, economic factors exerted greater pressure on this model. Monumental collection building as a societal good or as a marker of university quality was no longer considered economically feasible, due to price inflation for print and electronic products, the increase in the production of scholarly material, and the increased cost of storing materials that might never circulate. Some libraries adopted the new paradigm of "just-in-time" (JIT) inventory, implemented in the Japanese auto industry in the 1980s. In the JIT model, a large inventory of parts is viewed as waste. Instead, only the minimal inventory is maintained on site. In a library context, inventory consists of materials purchased in anticipation of future need. A large inventory of materials that never circulate is viewed as waste because it costs money to maintain and does not produce a product. This problem can be avoided by not buying library materials until there is a patron request. This JIT paradigm was tested in the 1990s through interlibrary loan (ILL) purchase-on-demand programs.

INTERLIBRARY LOAN PURCHASE ON DEMAND: ILPOD AT OSUL

In 1990, Bucknell University began purchasing books requested by patrons through ILL if it was faster or more economical than borrowing. The pilot was so successful that Bucknell's ILL department was incorporated into their acquisitions department (Perdue and Van Fleet 1999; Ward et al. 2003). Other libraries adopted this model under various names, e.g., purchase on demand, direct purchase, just-in-time acquisitions, patron-demand acquisitions, and patron-initiated collection development. All libraries established criteria to determine which items should be purchased or borrowed. These criteria generally included cost, publication date, availability to borrow or purchase the item, turnaround time, level of scholarship, and the borrower's status (Zopfi-Jordan 2008, 389; Allen et al. 2003; Ward 2002, 95). Librarians continued to mediate the process; not all patron requests were turned into purchases.

OSUL's interlibrary loan purchase on demand (ILPOD) evolved from a 2008 test called "Search OSU and Beyond," in which the OSUL homepage search box directed queries to the WorldCat database. OSUL and OhioLINK holdings were displayed at the top of the search results. Because patrons were searching a larger database, they were more likely to retrieve results, but fewer of the items were held by OSUL or by OhioLINK consortium members. A link to ILL prompted patrons to request non-OhioLINK titles. As soon as the "Search OSU and Beyond" service started, OSUL's head of interlibrary services noticed an increase in ILL requests, especially for new publications, textbooks, and forthcoming items found in WorldCat.

The OSUL head of interlibrary services worked with the monographs department, and later with a subject librarian who reviewed requests, to establish an ILL purchase-on-demand program. The program was not advertised to patrons. Instead, patrons received an e-mail saying the item they had requested through ILL was being purchased and would soon be available for their use. Requests were rush-ordered and monographs department staff e-mailed the patron when the item arrived. The speed of supply and personal notification made this ongoing program popular with patrons.

The librarian responsible for mediating ILPOD requests used her judgment before forwarding a title for ordering. The general criteria she established included the following:

- $200 price limit
- Publication date in the last two years
- Preference for scholarly material
- Items that OSUL was unable to borrow
- Media and foreign language requests were allowed
- Textbooks were allowed, which supplemented the OSUL Textbook Project, with a budget of $10,000 per year to purchase textbooks to be put on closed reserve
- Computer manuals, popular culture materials, and fiction were excluded unless the patron indicated the item was needed for classroom or research purposes
- Exceptions were made as judgment calls

In the 22 months between March 2008 and December 2009, the ILPOD liaison fielded 2,146 requests forwarded from ILL, resulting in 560 purchases (26% of ILL titles referred) at a cost of $68,297. ILPOD was funded centrally, not by subject funds. Among the items not purchased were 68 not-yet-published titles, which were referred to subject specialists, and 121 out of 243 requested textbooks. Other items were borrowed through ILL. The most frequent beneficiaries of ILPOD were graduate students (47%), followed by undergraduates (25%), faculty (20%), and staff (8%). ILPOD purchases averaged 16 circulations: a high number, considering the oldest item had been owned for only 22 months. The highest circulation was a textbook, soon placed on closed reserve, with 151 circulations. As reported by other libraries, ILPOD requests appear to circulate at a higher rate than the general collections (Comer and Lorenzen 2005; Chan 2004). The paradigm at OSUL is slowly shifting from just-in-case collection development by librarians to more JIT librarian-mediated purchases that respond to patron requests at point of need. The next phase in this paradigm shift involves the introduction of unmediated patron-initiated collection development.

EBRARY PILOT PROJECTS AT OSUL

2008 was a watershed year for integrating e-book acquisitions into mainstream academic library workflows. In that year, the two major book vendors, Blackwell and YBP, adapted their ordering databases, Collection Manager and GOBI, respectively, to supply e-books from aggregators OCLC NetLibrary, EBL, and ebrary. This was a welcome alternative to negotiating separate licenses with individual publishers. These GOBI e-book orders followed the traditional model of selection by librarians, although some e-books were purchased for the ILPOD program based on patron requests.

Doug Way briefly summarized the situation faced by many libraries: "... in the past six years only 31% of the library's book collection has circulated. At the same time there has been a dramatic increase in the use of ILL.... Seeing the use of ILL as an indicator of unmet demand, the library began to look toward patron-initiated collecting as a way to identify works that would enhance the library's collections" (Way 2009, 303). OSUL was also interested in meeting patron needs while increasing the number of times a title circulated.

The monographs department received administrative approval in 2009 to test ebrary's new patron-driven access service and established a deposit account of $25,000 with ebrary. In September 2009, ebrary provided approximately 93,000 e-book titles in an Excel spreadsheet that listed the ebrary ID number, title, author, publisher, content owner, LC call number, print ISBN, eISBN, two non-LC subject headings, and list price. The head of the monographs department used criteria recommended by the OSUL Collections Advisory Council (CAC) to reduce the number of records. The criteria *excluded* the following:

- Pre-2007 imprints
- List price over $299.99
- Forty publishers (not wanted or already acquired via standing orders or OhioLINK)
- Twenty subject headings (e.g., Juvenile Fiction, Self-Help)

- Computer manuals
- Technical areas in law
- Foreign language texts with no English language content
- Fiction (literary fiction and short stories were included)

Applying these criteria reduced the spreadsheet to fewer than 16,000 titles. The spreadsheet was returned to ebrary staff along with detailed criteria for types of materials to be excluded. Ebrary used this profile, similar to that of an approval plan, to generate a file of full MARC records, and OSUL staff downloaded the records from ebrary's Web site. This group of about 16,000 librarian-mediated e-books constituted the Test 1 database.

The loading of Test 1 records into the OSUL catalog took about one week. First, a load table was created in OSUL's Innovative Interfaces, Inc. Millennium system so an item record with fixed field data would be attached to the incoming bibliographic records. Before the load, MarcEdit was used to move and add data. The URL from the MARC 856 was moved to the local 956 field. Records were coded to display in the OSUL catalog but were not contributed to OhioLINK or WorldCat. A 910 field was added to identify test records, including the date of the load. Test 1 records in the public catalog looked identical to other e-book holdings, except that they lacked a call number. Patrons clicked on a "Connect to Resource" link and went directly to the full text of the e-book hosted on ebrary's server, identical to the procedure and display of other ebrary e-books owned by OSUL. There was no indication that the e-book was part of a test or that patron use would trigger a purchase. The test was not advertised to patrons. Test 1 went live October 25, 2009. OSUL librarians hoped the $25,000 deposit would be sufficient for the full 18-week test, so everyone was surprised when ebrary staff notified OSUL that the deposit had been expended in a little over four weeks. Statistics supplied by ebrary showed that patrons began triggering purchases on the first day, which was a Sunday. During Test 1, ebrary set OSUL's trigger for purchase at ten "activities." An "activity" occurred when a patron views a page not previously viewed or prints or copies any page of the e-book. Purchases ranged from a daily low of 5 to a high of 22, but averaged 12 per day at a cost of about $1,150 per day. Test 1 was frozen at the end of 37 days, on November 30, 2009. Patrons had triggered a total of 450 titles for purchase, and additional funds were needed to retain all the triggered titles. At OSUL's request, ebrary turned off access to non-purchased titles, and OSUL suppressed the unpurchased MARC records from public view.

The head of the monographs department and members of CAC reviewed the patron-driven access purchases. A question soon arose concerning imprint dates; several of the titles purchased were older than 2007. ebrary staff discovered that metadata supplied by some publishers listed the e-book release date, not the date of the original content. Publishers had mined their backlists for new e-books; patrons, who could see accurate imprint dates in the MARC records, had purchased titles published twenty or more years before the 2007 through 2009 profile dates. ebrary agreed to "unpurchase" these titles after a list was provided.

The ebrary representatives were helpful in resolving each issue with OSUL, discussing what was learned from Test 1 in light of future options. One discussion was how to restrict costs by further reducing the overall number of patron-driven access titles to exclude lower-use items that still triggered a purchase. To make that reduction, it was necessary to understand which e-books would be used most heavily by patrons and would thus be the most cost-effective purchases. Were the criteria used too broad? Should OSUL have already acquired these titles? Would librarians have purchased these titles with their subject funds? If so, should a portion of acquisitions funds be shifted to patron-initiated purchases? Or were patrons triggering titles that were unsuitable for an academic library? Data were analyzed to answer these questions.

USE OF TEST 1 AND TEST 2 E-BOOKS BY SUBJECT

Although a program offering fewer patron-driven access titles would help limit fiscal liability, it would also decrease patron access to e-book content. The ebrary staff offered an interesting alternative. Why not test an unmediated group of titles to see whether patron use differed substantially? OSUL and ebrary agreed that this second test of patron activity would use ebrary's Academic Complete database, representing about 43,000 e-books with imprint dates ranging from 1866 to 2009. This group of records was called Test 2 and ran for 37 days to match the length of Test 1. ebrary provided the MARC records, which were again edited and loaded into the OSUL catalog for patron discovery. At the end of Test 2, ebrary provided raw data for the authors to analyze.

Some OSUL librarians assumed that patrons in the sciences were more apt to use e-books than were patrons in the humanities or social sciences. In Test 1, patrons triggered more science titles (40%) than social science (33%) or humanities titles (27%). Test 1, however, involved a librarian-mediated selection of about 16,000 titles from a list of 93,000 titles. It is possible the selection process favored the inclusion of more science and social science titles. The unmediated file in Test 2 showed a different pattern. A total of 1,242 of the 43,000 titles in Test 2 were viewed by patrons. Social science titles were viewed most heavily (39%), followed by humanities (37%), and sciences (24%). It was not possible to analyze the huge record sets to see whether these differences were a function of how many titles in each subject were added to the catalog. Preliminary findings, however, show that OSUL patrons in the humanities and social sciences were as apt to use e-books as patrons in the sciences.

TABLE 1 Test 1 Titles Triggered for Purchase by Subject

Subjects	No. of Titles Purchased	% of All Titles Purchased
Health Sciences	52	11.6
Business/Economics	46	10.2
Psychology	30	6.7
Education/Physical Education	27	6.0
Engineering	23	5.1
Agriculture/Natural Resources	22	4.9
History	19	4.2
English	18	4.0
Biological Sciences	15	3.3
Mathematics/Statistics	15	3.3
Sociology/Social Work	15	3.3
Chemistry	14	3.1
Political Science	14	3.1
All other subjects*	140	31.2
Total	450	100%

*All other subjects have ≤3% of total titles purchased.

Table 1 and Table 2 outline patron use by subject. Subjects were assigned by one of the authors. Due to the number of multidisciplinary titles, some OSUL subject specialists did not agree with the more than 40 subject assignments made. However, the assignment of subjects between Test 1 and Test 2 should be relatively uniform because they were assigned by the same person.

Data show that the unmediated ebrary Academic Complete database in Test 2 resulted in higher usage of social science and humanities titles. Data also show that the number of subjects viewed in Test 2 was more diverse than in Test 1. All subjects less than or equal to 3% of the total titles viewed represent 43.7% in Test 2, but only 31.2% in Test 1. Again, this may be a

TABLE 2 Test 2 Titles Viewed by Subject

Subjects	No. of Titles Viewed	% of All Titles Viewed
Education/Physical Education	189	15.2
Business/Economics	105	8.5
Health Sciences	94	7.6
English	87	7.0
Sociology/Social Work	51	4.1
History	49	3.9
Psychology	49	3.9
Political Science	39	3.1
Biological Sciences	37	3.0
All other subjects*	542	43.7
Total	1,242	100%

*All other subjects have ≤3% of total titles viewed.

function of the criteria used to create the Test 1 database. Both tests took place during comparable weeks in fall and winter quarter. No advertising was done for either test, so the increase in use can be attributed to the larger number of titles in the Test 2 database and to the fact that Test 2 counted all titles viewed, not just those exceeding the ten "activity" trigger in Test 1.

USE OF E-BOOKS BY IMPRINT DATE

The Test 1 database was supposed to be restricted to 2007 to 2009 imprints, although the sample had earlier imprints, as noted. Print edition dates were later assigned to Test 1 data to ensure accuracy and comparability with Test 2. The error in creating the sample revealed that patrons, who saw only the accurate MARC record imprint dates in the catalog, were knowingly using older imprints. In Test 1, 10% of the titles purchased were published from 1987 to 2006 and 28% were published in 2007, 32% in 2008, and 31% in 2009. The imprint range in Test 2 was much broader, ranging from 1866 to 2009, due to inclusion of backlist titles. Table 3 lists the imprint range of the 1,242 titles viewed by patrons in Test 2.

Table 3 shows that there was still interest in older books. Indeed, the number of books viewed (542) from 2000 to 2004 exceeded the number (513) from 2005 to 2009. However, because of the differing total number of books available in each range, the percentage of older books viewed was consistently lower than the percentage of newer books viewed. These data show that imprint date is a predictor of patron use of e-books.

TEST 1 AND TEST 2 RESULTS BY PUBLISHER TYPE

Test 1 excluded a substantial number of publishers, some because OSUL acquired their titles through OhioLINK group purchases (e.g., Springer) and some because of the level or type of titles published. Many smaller presses

TABLE 3 Test 2 Patron Use by Imprint Year

Imprint Year	No. of Titles in Database	% of All Titles in Database	No. of Titles Viewed by Patrons	% of Titles Viewed by Patrons
1866–1989	923	2.1	19	2.06
1990–1994	1,674	3.8	29	1.73
1995–1999	6,136	14.0	139	2.27
2000–2004	21,365	49.0	542	2.54
2005–2009	13,563	31.1	513	3.78
Totals	43,661	100%	1,242	2.84

TABLE 4 Categories of Titles Purchased in Test 1 or Viewed in Test 2

Type of Work	Test 1: No. and% of Titles Purchased	Test 2: No. and% of Titles Viewed
Intermediate–advanced	230 (51.1%)	734 (59.1%)
Introductory	67 (14.9%)	364 (29.3%)
Professional	41 (9.1%)	24 (2.0%)
Textbooks/all levels	38 (8.4%)	34 (2.7%)
General/reference	21 (4.7%)	10 (0.8%)
Multidisciplinary	21 (4.7%)	31 (2.5%)
Testing/study aids	21 (4.7%)	17 (1.4%)
Serial volumes	7 (1.5%)	14 (1.1%)
Career materials	4 (0.9%)	14 (1.1%)
Totals	450 (100%)	1,242 (100%)

were excluded to cut the overall number. Patron use by publisher type for Test 1 was, therefore, a factor of the set of records provided to users. Results reflect this: trade publishers including medical publishers (79%), university presses (20%), associations and organizations (1%), and small publishers (<1%). In Test 2, when the entire ebrary Academic Complete database was used, results were as follows: trade publishers including medical publishers (47%), university presses (33%), associations and organizations (15%), and small publishers (6%). This distribution of types of publishers in Test 2 reflects patrons' needs more accurately than the distribution in Test 1.

OSUL librarians were interested in knowing the types or categories (i.e., audience level, treatment) of e-books used by patrons. These categories, however, were not assigned by ebrary, and there were insufficient resources to research each title, so one of the authors subjectively assigned categories to the 450 titles purchased in Test 1 and the 1,242 titles viewed by patrons in Test 2 (see Table 4). The textbook category, if it was not clear from the title, was assigned to any title that had a high number of subsequent editions.

NUMBER OF USER LOGINS AND AMOUNT OF E-BOOK READ

Test 1 data (see Table 5) show that of the 450 titles purchased, patrons viewed a total of 18,567 pages, of which 11,866 were unique pages; 2,791 pages were

TABLE 5 Number of Activities for Titles in Test 1

Titles purchased (≥10 activities)	450
Pages viewed	18,567
Pages printed	2,791
Pages copied	193
Total activities	21,551
Average activities per title	48

TABLE 6 Number of Activities for Titles in Test 2

Titles viewed (≥1 activity)	1,242
Pages viewed	44,442
Pages printed	6,123
Pages copied	304
Total activities	50,889
Average activities per title	41

printed and 193 pages were copied for a total of 21,551 "activities" (total activities = pages viewed + pages printed + pages copied). The highest number of pages viewed from a single title was 356 pages. The average number of activities per title was 48. This level of use suggested more than casual browsing.

Test 2 included data on all 1,242 titles viewed (see Table 6). It should be noted that 618 (50%) of the titles had fewer than ten activities, a use level not counted in Test 1. The other 624 titles, with ten or more activities, however, showed heavy use, including 16 titles in the range of 500 to 2,373 activities. The most often used title, a 1999 imprint, had 1,787 pages viewed and 581 pages printed over 148 login sessions.

There was concern that a single patron could trigger purchase of an excessive number of titles. Although it was not possible to identify whether one or more individuals accessed a title in either test, it was possible to count activity (viewed, copied, printed) in Test 1 and to count the number of login sessions plus activity in Test 2. A review of titles in both tests showed that no more than two books on the same subject were triggered or accessed on any given day, so this concern appears unfounded.

OSUL AND OHIOLINK HOLDINGS OF PATRON-DRIVEN ACCESS PURCHASES

Test 1 resulted in 450 titles purchased, which were then searched in the OSUL and OhioLINK catalogs to determine whether sufficient print copies were already available, a figure set at OSUL as five available circulating copies in OhioLINK. Nine percent of the purchased e-books had no holdings in OhioLINK; 65% had zero to four available copies and would have met OSUL's criteria for firm orders. The "ineligible" 35% resulted from the inability to remove duplicates before the tests.

To see whether OSUL patrons continued to use older print editions because newer editions had not been purchased until the patron-driven access test, the 450 purchased e-books were searched to see whether OSUL held an earlier print edition. In 42 cases, an earlier print edition was found;

when the circulation records of these items were examined, 28 of them had circulated in the last two years. These recently circulated print editions were on average 12 years older than the e-book editions purchased by patrons during the patron-driven access test, showing that OSUL patrons continued to use outdated print editions before later electronic editions were purchased and raising concerns about currency of the collections.

SUBJECT LIBRARIANS' COMMENTS ON PATRON-DRIVEN ACCESS PURCHASES

The authors polled subject librarians on whether they would have used their subject funds to buy titles purchased by patrons in Test 1. Most agreed they would have, but several concerns were raised. Some subject librarians commented on the problem of duplication, and the authors agreed that an ongoing patron-driven access program must have a way to exclude titles already owned in print to save money for unique content. One librarian was concerned with imprint dates: "The 2009 titles would be likely candidates for purchase, but earlier out-of-date titles might not have been included. From my perspective, currency is of prime value when selecting electronic copy." This comment was of interest to the authors because test data showed that OSUL patrons were using both pre-2007 e-books and even older print editions, because they were available for discovery in the catalog. The authors do not agree that e-books published prior to 2009 are out of date, any more than a pre-2009 print title is necessarily out of date. The authors see this comment as an example of differing expectations for e-books and for print books. Even though content was identical, the delivery system generated differing expectations.

Another concern was funding and whether book funds should be used for so many different levels of materials. The authors are concerned that, if subject funds are limited, they would be used exclusively for upper-level research materials. The entire materials budget is insufficient to cover upper-level research material to support all of OSU's 160 major programs and 63,200 students at a comprehensive level; the expertise of the subject librarian is vital in selecting the best new and retrospective items to support patrons' needs. The authors' position is that lower-level undergraduates, especially freshmen, would be underserved if only advanced titles were purchased. New undergraduates are the population least likely to wait for a book to be borrowed from another OhioLINK library, even if they are aware that borrowing is an option. Undergraduates may especially benefit from a patron-driven access model that purchases "hot topic" or introductory books for term papers with short deadlines. Instant online access is a method familiar to younger students.

ROLE OF COLLECTION DEVELOPMENT LIBRARIANS IN THE AGE OF PATRON-DRIVEN ACCESS

The potential for a gap between the collection building philosophy of librarians and the immediate information needs of freshmen, undergraduates, and other library users is the crux of the paradigm shift from librarian-mediated to patron-initiated purchasing. Patrons in both tests were using materials at point of need. These included lower-level, introductory, and cross-disciplinary works as well as more focused upper-level and professional-level works. Subject librarians, on the other hand, generally focus on using finite funds to buy works of high quality to cover subjects needed to support teaching and research. There is a real difference between building a balanced collection for the future and giving patrons what they want now. There is a realistic concern that patrons, in buying for immediate need, will change the nature of academic collections over time, generating excessive amounts of purchases in one area to the detriment of building a balanced collection. Patron-initiated collection development might also polarize collection levels between introductory works and narrowly focused research materials with less variation in between. How many of these concerns are real can only be determined through further study.

The question of purchasing books in interdisciplinary areas or introductory level publications will continue to be a factor in the paradigm shift from librarian-mediated to patron-initiated collection development. As Nora Rawlinson noted in her 1981 article, "Give 'Em What They Want!" a "book of outstanding quality is not worth its price if no one will read it" (Rawlinson, 2188). Certainly, a patron-driven access model gives patrons what they want. The question is whether a library can afford to pay for what patrons want using currently existing patron-driven access business models. For example, during Test 1, OSUL patrons triggered purchases at the rate of about $1,150 per day over 37 days from a database of about 16,000 e-books. Extrapolating those figures, an OSUL patron-driven access program would cost about $418,000 per year. It is unlikely that OSUL subject libraries would be willing to turn such a large proportion of the acquisitions budget over to patrons when they already feel their budgets are insufficient.

Are collection development librarians obsolete in the age of patron-initiated acquisitions? Considering the realities of the e-book marketplace, the answer is a resounding "no." Even the largest e-book aggregators have rights to distribute only a fraction of the titles published each year in the United States. The content available through patron-driven access programs, although valuable in fulfilling immediate need, is a small subset of what is published. An academic research library requires more content than current e-book aggregators can provide, just as it requires more content than a single domestic approval plan can provide. The building of an academic research library is still dependent on the expertise of subject librarians.

CONCLUSION

A paradigm shift is underway to allow greater patron input into e-books acquired by academic libraries based on use. This can be seen through ILPOD and patron-driven acquisition programs. The pilot programs at OSUL examined two ebrary e-book tests. Some of the findings showed that patrons in the sciences, social sciences, and humanities were all active users of e-books during the tests; imprint date was a major predictor of e-book use, although many older imprints showed high usage; patron-triggered purchases varied by level from introductory works, study guides, and multidisciplinary titles to advanced professional literature; and the majority of titles purchased as a result of patron use showed more than one login session and relatively high use.

The findings also point to issues that need to be addressed in the marketplace and by individual libraries: if patron-driven access e-book programs are to be sold to libraries, the amount of patron use that triggers a purchase must be set far higher than present models; patron-driven access products must have real-time monitoring of use and ongoing expenditures to prevent runaway costs; libraries will need to restrict the number and type of titles offered to patrons and develop some model of how to do this; and libraries will want to set priorities for the role patron-initiated purchasing will play in their overall acquisitions program.

The library of the electronic age should provide both the option to "give 'em what they want now" and to acquire items that may be needed later. To ignore an immediate patron need is to go against the library's role to support its constituents. To provide only immediately needed items is to ignore the reality that some just-in-case content must be purchased, otherwise it will not be available when it is needed.

REFERENCES

Allen, Megan, Suzanne M. Ward, Tanner Wray, and Karl E. Debus-Lopez. 2003. Patron-focused services in three US libraries: Collaborative interlibrary loan, collection development and acquisitions. *Interlending & Document Supply 31*(2): 138–141.

Chan, Gayle Rosemary Y. C. 2004. Purchase instead of borrow: An international perspective. *Journal of Interlibrary Loan Document Delivery and Information Supply 14*: 23–38.

Comer, Alberta, and Elizabeth Lorenzen. 2005. Biz of ACQ–Is purchase-on-demand a worthy model? Do patrons really know what they want? *Against the Grain* (February): 75–78.

Perdue, Jennifer, and James A. Van Fleet. 1999. Borrow or buy? Cost-effective delivery of monographs. *Journal of Interlibrary Loan, Document Delivery & Information Supply 9*(4): 19–28.

Rawlinson, Nora. 1981. "Give 'em what they want!" *Library Journal 106*(20): 2188–2190.

Ward, Suzanne M. 2002. Books on demand: Just-in-time acquisitions. *Acquisitions Librarian 27*: 95–107.

Ward, Suzanne M., Tanner Wray, and Karl E. Debus-López. 2003. Collection development based on patron requests: Collaboration between interlibrary loan and acquisitions. *Library Collections, Acquisitions, and Technical Services 27*(2): 203–213.

Way, Doug. 2009. The assessment of patron-initiated collection development via interlibrary loan at a comprehensive university. *Journal of Interlibrary Loan, Document Delivery & Electronic Reserve 19*(4): 299–308.

Zopfi-Jordan, David. 2008. Purchasing or borrowing: Making interlibrary loan decisions that enhance patron satisfaction. *Journal of Interlibrary Loan, Document Delivery & Electronic Reserve 18*(3): 387–394.

Point-of-Need Collection Development: The Getting It System Toolkit (GIST) and a New System for Acquisitions and Interlibrary Loan Integrated Workflow and Collection Development

KATE PITCHER, TIM BOWERSOX, CYRIL OBERLANDER, and MARK SULLIVAN

State University of New York, Geneseo, New York

The authors developed the Getting It System Toolkit (GIST) software, which integrates with the commercially available ILLiad interlibrary loan (ILL) management software. At the point that a user places an ILL request or a book purchase request, GIST collects information from both the user and from external sources to provide decision-making data, such as whether the title is held locally, whether a free Internet version exists, whether the user has a format or edition preference, and how much the title costs. Working together, GIST and ILLiad simplify the complex ILL and acquisitions processes by allowing loan and purchase requests to pass between the two departments. GIST is an innovative tool designed to reconcile formerly disparate workflows and enable effective collection decision making.

INTRODUCTION

The State University of New York (SUNY) College at Geneseo is a small undergraduate school where the teaching faculty historically selected the

The work was partially funded by a Regional Bibliographic Database grant through the generosity of the Rochester Regional Library Council in Rochester, NY.

bulk of print materials for the library collection. The library faculty members' collection development responsibilities focused on developing and maintaining the reference collection. SUNY Geneseo's Milne Library interlibrary loan (ILL) department, called Information Delivery Services (IDS), is heavily used, handling nearly 30,000 borrowing requests in fiscal year 2008–2009 (19,597 loans and 10,297 articles). Such high levels of ILL requests clearly indicate an unmet demand for materials within the local campus community.

The dual situations of collection development by teaching faculty and high ILL borrowing statistics helped drive the creation of a new collection development paradigm and workflow. The cornerstone of the new system is ILLiad, the ILL/document delivery management software from OCLC/Atlas Systems that Milne Library already used. ILLiad is exceptionally flexible and customizable. Requests are routed into various queues, either automatically, when the requests meet certain preset criteria, or by staff. As just two examples, a library might create a custom queue for requests that need further bibliographic verification or for requests that need certain specialized checking, such as in the British Library's online catalog. Staff then process similar requests in one session; after processing, the requests move into new queues, such as one with records of items that have yet to arrive. Multiple staff members can access ILLiad simultaneously. Staff can also create templates to send e-mail messages to users; many messages will be identical, such as those notifying patrons that the titles they requested are available in the local collection. In addition, users can check their own ILLiad accounts to view the status of any current requests.

Users are central to the new collection development paradigm at Milne Library and other libraries. As library collections and space are under increased scrutiny, actual use is the main determinant of sustained support. This factor offers a suite of relevant critical issues to the future of selection and collections: expensive just-in-case collection development models have produced collections that have roughly 50% usage and require an expensive deselection process much later on; collection space is seen in conflict with the need to increase user spaces; user-initiated selection is a better predictor for continued use than just-in-case models (Ward 2002); and disparate interfaces that only make sense to libraries and librarians, not users, only impede the purchase and ILL request process.

TRANSFORMING THE DECISION MAKING AND SELECTION WORKFLOW

For many ILL requests, it would be more cost-effective to buy the items from an online bookseller and add them to the collection after the ILL patrons' use, rather than to borrow the items though ILL and pay more expensive borrowing fees and return shipping costs. In a study of 110 book and media borrowing requests received in one day at SUNY Geneseo on April 6, 2008, one of the authors found that 87 items (79%) could be purchased from Amazon. Used copies of all these 87 titles could have been purchased for $2,224.71 ($25.57 per item), while all but three could have been purchased new for $2,851.27 ($32.77 per item). Over one-third could have been bought used for less than $10.00 each, and over one-fifth could be purchased new for less than $10.00 each. Overall, 46% could have been purchased for less than the Association of Research Libraries (ARL) unit cost for borrowing of $17.50 (Jackson 2004; Reighart and Oberlander 2008). In an age where monographs are no longer scarce resources and turnaround times for acquisitions are equal to those for ILL, librarians must create strategies that leverage data to help decide when to buy and when to borrow (Houle 2003; Perdue and Van Fleet 1999). However, expecting ILL staff to purchase more than a few specialized items outside the normal ILL workflow makes little sense: not only can their expertise be better used in borrowing items that the library decides not to buy, but there is already a department devoted to the purchasing process: acquisitions.

SUNY Geneseo library staff designed and implemented the Getting It System Toolkit (GIST) software in 2009 to work with ILLiad. GIST's goal was to transform the business of borrowing, buying, and accessing library materials in two important ways. The first way was to integrate ILL and acquisitions into one flexible workflow. GIST requests may follow a borrowing or a purchasing path; using ILLiad, staff can easily route requests between ILL and acquisitions depending on a number of factors, such as user recommendations, the borrowing cost versus the purchase price, regional library holdings, and more. The second way was to automate the integration of data to support librarians' decisions. The GIST system integrates with ILLiad to combine data from various vendor Web application programming interface (API) services with user request parameters, such as embedded questions about the acceptability of an electronic version. Staff can view all these data, automatically collected from both patrons and from selected external sources, on one screen to aid in deciding whether to buy or borrow each title (see Figure 1).

Cooperative Efforts and Leveraging Strengths

The GIST project started with ILL, acquisition, and collection development librarians at SUNY Geneseo working together to transform systems and workflow. Librarians agreed to stop fragmenting the library Web site around library departments and to redesign the request interface to focus on users' needs. The GIST request interface was a modification of the existing ILL request pages, but it now asked for feedback from users. For example, users are asked whether they recommend the item for purchase or for ILL, as well as

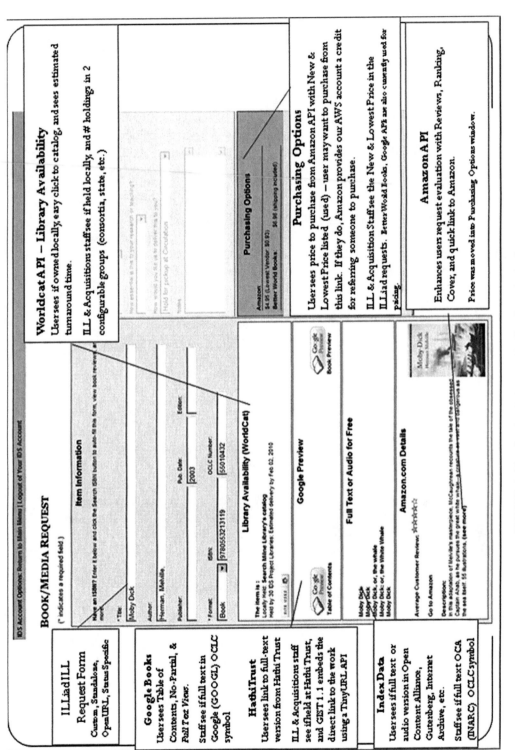

FIGURE 1 The Getting It System Toolkit (GIST) interface.

being asked about delivery options. To work effectively, ILL and acquisitions needed to share a robust and flexible request system that processed requests using real-time cost-benefit analysis. For example, within the ILLiad client it became possible for acquisitions and ILL librarians to evaluate each request alongside user feedback, regional holdings, and purchase prices to make effective buy or borrow decisions. A shared workflow required developing a customized set of request queues, user notifications, and routing options. Fortunately, ILLiad both met all the criteria and offered an added community dimension, as local developments could be useful to over a thousand other libraries that already use this software.

Traditionally, both ILL and acquisitions departments created workflows that involved complex, time-consuming, and cost-intensive tasks for searching, verifying, and ordering materials for patrons (Ward et al. 2003). Using ILLiad as the hybrid ILL and acquisition request management software, the GIST Web interface was designed as a set of adaptable workflow tools to make the request information interoperable with only one click, eliminating many manual searching processes.

DATA-SUPPORTED STRATEGIES AND INTERDEPENDENT DECISION-MAKING

Cost, format, publication dates, and turnaround times are all part of the criteria used to decide when it makes sense to borrow or buy, much like an approval plan; this strategy for a transformed workflow focuses on the user's requirements and what the library wants to do about them, regardless of where the request entered the system (Reighart and Oberlander 2008).

GIST's tools are designed to enhance both the user's request experience and the library's ILL service and purchase request system, as well as to transform collection development and resource sharing. Using GIST eliminates the former manual processes in both ILL and acquisitions of making a series of searches in various vendor platforms to obtain all the information needed to make a borrowing or a buying decision. The criteria used in developing GIST included data from which both users and library staff benefit.

Building GIST

GIST is a comprehensive request interface that allows the user to make many of the decisions that have traditionally been handled behind the scenes. To build this system, in early spring 2009, four members of SUNY Geneseo's Milne Library staff redesigned the existing purchase request form. The Rochester Regional Library Council (RRLC) funded the project. Among many processes, the development phases included gathering design requirements from other libraries, faculty discussions, and a literature review; developing the ILLiad interface; customizing Web pages; and integrating Amazon Web services, Google Books, and WorldCat API and other data programming.

In addition to submitting requests, the interface also allows users to make decisions about delivery while expanding their options (for instance, going directly to the vendor to purchase the item themselves). GIST ultimately gives users and library staff similar and customizable data about the request to provide each with the information needed to make informed decisions easily. In the GIST request interface, a user submits the request using the ILLiad request form, either supplying citation information manually or utilizing OpenURL. Several streams of information are automatically retrieved; the most important of these are holdings information, full text availability, pricing and purchasing information, and user preferences. Using the WorldCat API, the patron and library staff are able to see holdings availability for custom groups. SUNY Geneseo librarians created three custom groups depending on whether items are held locally, by preferred consortia, or by other in-state libraries. For titles owned locally, users see a direct link to the item in the catalog. Second, if an item is held within the IDS Project, the library cooperative to which the SUNY Geneseo library belongs, users see the number of holdings and a customizable statement that estimates the delivery date. The request goes to an ILLiad queue for acquisitions review if the consortial holdings are below a configurable threshold. Finally, titles falling into the third group of items held in New York State or in the coordinated collection development group are routed to a processing queue for library staff to make decisions about whether to purchase a book depending upon how many copies are already available within a particular network.

This routing effectively reduces the amount of duplication already present within particular groups of libraries. Library staff members have all the holdings data immediately available within the ILLiad client to route requests, such as e-mailing users or the selectors who review titles for potential purchase or transferring requests between the acquisitions and ILL workflows. The customizable holdings groups enable acquisitions, collection development, and other staff members to make quick decisions about whether to purchase an item, depending on how many copies exist in the second and/or third groups. Requests automatically route to an ILLiad queue for ILL processing if consortial holdings exceed a certain limit, or they route to a different queue to suggest a purchase if consortial holdings are low. At Geneseo, for example, staff created a queue for fulfilling requests via ILL when there were four or more copies within the cooperative network. Any request for a title with fewer than four network holdings automatically goes into a special queue; staff members review these requests and the accompanying data to make a purchase decision. Users receive e-mails when titles are selected for purchase. If staff decide not to buy a title, the request moves back into the ILL processing queue.

Staff members direct users to free, full-text content online whenever possible. The GIST interface automatically searches several Internet sites checking for this free, full-text content. The Google Books API retrieves matching titles and gives users a link to full-text, content preview, or table of contents. The Index Data API shows the user any full-text or audio version available from many digital repositories and archives, including Internet Archive, Open Content Alliance, and Project Gutenberg. The HathiTrust API connects users to full-text versions available in this federated digital library. This GIST component is used in conjunction with a TinyURL API to automate not only the detection of full-text for the user, but also to create a small URL that populates the ILLiad client for use by acquisitions and ILL staff. From the ILLiad staff view, the associated OCLC code displays whenever it is available.

Similar to the routing processes based upon local and regional holdings, data from these Web sources enable staff to route all incoming requests with full-text online versions to a special queue. Since the request interface prompts users for format preferences, staff members notify users of the online version when this format is acceptable, rather than processing an ILL loan request or considering the title for purchase. GIST is set up to send automatic e-mail to the electronic resources cataloging librarian who usually adds the free online title to the local catalog for others to discover. As an example, Table 1 shows five requests filled with referrals to full-text documents in HathiTrust.

The Amazon API retrieves Amazon.com pricing information, the familiar star user ratings and recommendations, available reviews and previews, and a link to the full page on Amazon.com. Users can get pricing information from other vendors and publishers; they see multiple vendor prices (new and lowest) and other purchasing options. This information gives users the option of clicking a link that starts an item search with the vendors to purchase the item. Users can personally buy an item or place the request as an ILL or purchase request.

If the user submits a request, the acquisition and ILL staff also see the Amazon new and lowest prices in their client view. In many cases this information facilitates decision making because staff can immediately compare the costs of borrowing versus buying. Milne Library currently orders the bulk of materials through Amazon and YBP, so having instant access to pricing information is helpful for making quick decisions about where to purchase materials. Amazon's fast turnaround time makes it a favorite vendor for just-in-time purchases.

Several of the recent purchase-on-demand studies show turnaround times for acquisitions departments that are faster or comparable to turnaround times in ILL departments (Allen et al. 2003; Houle 2003), in many cases averaging seven to eight days. Brug and MacWaters (2004) specifically credit their choice of online booksellers with fast delivery times; vendor discounts are only a secondary consideration. For Milne Library, speed versus

TABLE 1 Examples of Requests Filled with Referrals to Full-Text Documents in HathiTrust

Loan Author	Loan Title	Date	Full Text TinyURL.com LINK	Amazon	Transaction Date	OCLC #	CCD	IDS	Dept.
Mann, Horace	Life and works of Horace Mann	1891	http://tinyurl.com/ylhtln9		2/12/2010	4316725	1	3	Unknown
Wemms, William	The trial of the British soldiers, of the 29th regiment of foot, for the murder of Crispus Attucks, Samuel Gray, Samuel Maverick, James Caldwell, and Patrick Carr, on Monday evening, March 5, 1770	1807	http://tinyurl.com/yeuyppp		2/12/2010	1699284	1	2	History
Quincy, Josiah	Memoir of the life of Josiah Quincy	1971	http://tinyurl.com/ybdwxqg	Amazon: $86.00	2/12/2010	131139	0	2	History
Moorman, Frederic	Robert Herrick, a biographical & critical study	1962	http://tinyurl.com/yzpwjsu		2/11/2010	230445	7	11	Chemistry
Adams, Samuel	The writings of Samuel Adams	1904	http://tinyurl.com/ycx7qyk		3/2/2010	1083711	10	17	History

cost was an important distinction; delivery time must be as fast or faster than ILL service.

Between GIST's implementation in September 2009 and February 2010, staff processed 529 purchase requests. The turnaround time averaged 14.56 days; the 2002 ARL study reported 9.29 days for mediated loan borrowing requests (Jackson 2003). Note that GIST selection criteria prefer unique titles within the region and that some purchasing requests include pre-publication titles. Turnaround time has improved since GIST was first implemented, dropping from 14.59 days in September 2009 to 7.34 days by December.

The request form offers users the chance to indicate their preferences on several variables, differing by patron status. Users indicate whether they want the item to be purchased for the library or processed via ILL. They can also indicate how essential the title is for their research or teaching. Delivery options, depending on user status, include holding the item for pick-up, shelving it in the library, or placing it on course reserve. The notes field lets users add information, such as course title, recommendations or reasons for purchasing, or information about funding the purchase. User indications about the acceptability of alternative formats or editions help staff determine whether newer editions or electronic full text would be acceptable.

Geneseo tested GIST with librarians and selected faculty in the late summer of 2009 and released it to all users by October 1, 2009. By March 1, 2010, 12,744 requests had been submitted through GIST. Of the 838 titles that users suggested for purchase, 529 (63%) were actually bought. An additional 16% were routed to ILL for fulfillment and 17% were cancelled for reasons such as too widely held within the local consortia, locally owned, or a required textbook. During the same time period, ILL converted 28 ILL requests to purchase items either because purchasing was less expensive than borrowing or because some titles were too new to borrow.

Over 30% of all the requests included optional information about the department affiliation and the importance of the book to users. Most users came from the departments of education (16%) or history (14%). The most frequently cited reasons for requesting the items were "essential for class or research" (19%) or "required textbook" (4%).

To summarize, GIST elicits helpful information from users while providing the library with key decision-making data from many sources, such as:

- Local and consortial holdings for cooperative collection development strategies
- Free online sources to fulfill requests promptly, to reduce costs, and to offer the option of cataloging these resources on a just-in-time basis
- Reviews and rankings to add value for users and to provide recommendations to selectors
- Purchasing options and prices to inform both users and library staff

The value-added work behind the scenes is done in the ILLiad software; library staff see a customized screen that integrates both ILL and acquisitions data in one screen but allows staff to route requests between departments.

GIST is easily customized. Some of the features include:

- Ability to turn components on or off easily
- If no data are available from any component, the style-sheet hides the component
- Ability to apply different API components to various ILLiad pages. For example, the stand-alone book request (non-OpenURL) has a search ISBN feature that populates the form based on supplying only the ISBN.
- The texts displayed for users and library staff are separately customizable. ILLiad offers customizable request forms by user status, which allows the text, options, and services to be tailored to the user's status.

IMPLEMENTING THE GIST WORKFLOW

Users quickly adopted the new GIST system because it was integrated into the existing ILL request system they were already using. However, the ILLiad software was new to acquisitions staff; they were trained to use it in August 2009 as the rollout began for all faculty. Best practices continue to develop in both acquisitions and ILL departments. See the Appendix for the GIST Acquisitions Workflow Map.

Essentially, the basic acquisitions workflow remains the same, but with key improvements. Using the ILLiad client, acquisitions now has one interface for managing all purchase requests. Purchase requests must be submitted through the GIST interface, either through the user's IDS (ILL) account, or from an OpenURL request. In the past, campus faculty submitted purchase requests using e-mail, written notes, flyers, torn pages from publishers' catalogs, and by phone or in person, but they have made a smooth transition to the GIST Web interface. Now all requests can be managed in one environment.

In the acquisitions workflow, all requests arrive first in ILLiad's Document Delivery module, which was designed to handle requests for materials the library owns or, in this case, may soon own. Within this environment, a custom view of the queues and requests was created to prioritize the acquisitions staff processing and hide the ILL processing (see Figure 2). Within ILLiad, custom queues were designed to follow local workflow, and certain routing rules (queries that will automatically change the status of requests based upon certain conditions) move the requests into them. For example, one of the acquisitions queues is named "purchase request exceeds CCD [Coordinated Collection Development] limit" because a routing rule has been

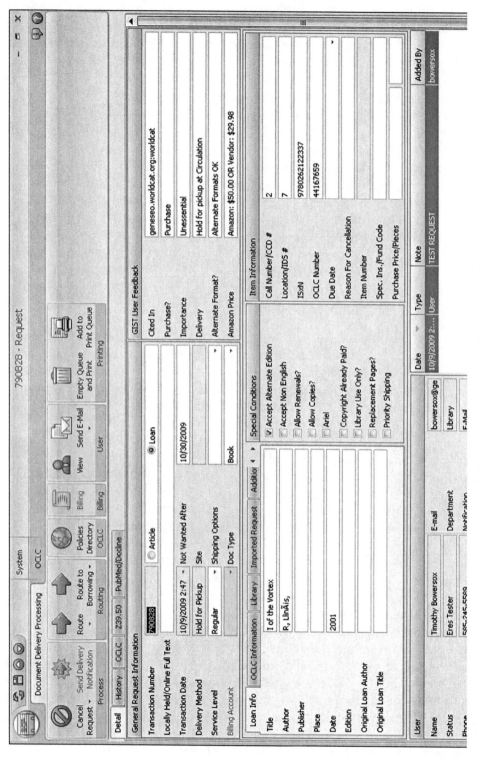

FIGURE 2 ILLIAD's document delivery module customized for acquisitions.

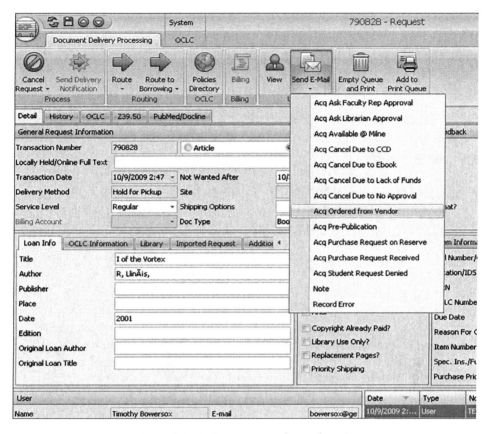

FIGURE 3 ILLIAD's customized e-mail routing.

written in ILLiad to route all purchase requests into this queue if four or more copies of that particular title are owned within the library network. No manual checking of holdings is required by staff; they can simply open the requests in this queue and determine whether to purchase the request. Then, with one click, staff can send a custom e-mail notification to the user. Milne Library has developed many custom acquisitions queues, such as "awaiting acquisitions processing," "purchase request ordered from vendor," and "awaiting faculty rep approval."

The custom queues, e-mail routing, and routing rules then determine how requests filter into each queue. E-mail routing is another ILLiad feature that was customized for the GIST workflow to streamline acquisitions processing. In addition to sending customizable e-mails from within ILLiad, with no need for staff to key in data, the ILLiad e-mails automatically advance requests through the workflow from start to finish. This process allows staff both to update a request's status and to e-mail the user simultaneously. The customized e-mails used by SUNY Geneseo's acquisitions include "purchase request received," "purchase request on reserve," "cancel due to lack of funds," "ask librarian approval," and others. These are tremendous time-savers over composing messages individually. Figure 3 shows an example of the ILLiad e-mail routing feature that facilitates staff sending notices to users.

CONCLUSIONS AND FUTURE DIRECTIONS

GIST compiles data about book and media requests that enable users and library staff to make informed decisions about purchases. The primary goals for the GIST project were to create a model for making user-initiated requests easier by merging acquisitions and ILL request workflows using one interface and by coordinating collection development and acquisition processing. Using ILLiad as a common request management tool, the newly developed GIST integrated several disparate information streams into one interface.

After transforming the acquisitions and ILL workflow, SUNY Geneseo librarians saw new possibilities for streamlining processes like gift management and deselection, as well as for creating new collection building strategies. For instance, during an upcoming massive de-selection of the education collection, staff will apply rapid collection building criteria to ILL requests to refresh this collection based on user input and the additional GIST data.

Over a thousand libraries currently use ILLiad as their ILL management software; all of them may consider applying GIST as a custom enhancement to various acquisitions and ILL processes. The authors welcome others' ideas for making GIST even more versatile in streamlining essential ILL and acquisitions processes.

The GIST team is working on developing more functionality to expand the features and tools for GIST version 2, scheduled for release in August 2010. The GIST2 project will add more vendor supplied APIs, including edition checking and some evaluative sources with trusted recommendations, book lists, and award notices.

Three new stand-alone tools will be added; two of these will be released as open source and do not require ILLiad. The gift manager streamlines gift acceptance and cataloging, including the ability to customize a conspectus for automatic recommendations to keep or discard gifts, as well as automatically creating donor letters. The deselection manager works with weeding projects either individually or in batch. The budget manager will work seamlessly with ILLiad to streamline acquisition ordering, capture invoices, manage budget funds, and automate purchasing.

ACKNOWLEDGEMENTS

The authors thank Adam Traub, St. John Fisher College, for beta testing; Kyle Banerjee, Alliance, and Terry Reese from Oregon State University, for

Worldcat API programming support; and Mike Flakus and Sherry Buchanan at Portland State University for the adaptation of the Amazon price grabber (http://digital.lib.pdx.edu/oss/apg).

FURTHER INFORMATION

GIST was released on August 15, 2009, under a Creative Commons license. For more information about GIST, a Web site with links to documentation and Listserv are available at http://idsproject.org/Tools/GIST.aspx.

REFERENCES

Allen, Megan, Suzanne M. Ward, Tanner Wray, and Karl E. Debus-Lopez. 2003. Patron-focused services in three US libraries: Collaborative interlibrary loan, collection development and acquisitions. *Interlending & Document Supply 31*(2): 138–141.

Brug, Sandy, and Cristi MacWaters. 2004. Patron-driven purchasing from interlibrary loan requests. *Colorado Libraries 30*(3): 36–38.

Houle, Louis. 2003. *Convergence between interlibrary loan and acquisitions: Can it be done?*, paper presented at 8th Interlending and Document Supply International Conference, Canberra, Australia, 28–31 October, available at: www.nla.gov.au/ilds/abstracts/convergencebetweeninterlibrary.htm (accessed 4 November 2009).

Jackson, Mary E. 2003. Assessing ILL/DD Services Study: Initial Observations. *ARL Bimonthly Report 230/231 October/December 2003*. Available at: http://www.arl.org/bm~doc/illdd.pdf (accessed May 25, 2010).

———. 2004. *Assessing ILL/DD services: New cost-effective alternatives*. Washington, DC: Association of Research Libraries, 9.

Perdue, Jennifer, and James A. Van Fleet. 1999. Borrow or buy: Cost-effective delivery of monographs. *Journal of Interlibrary Loan Document Delivery & Information Supply 9*(4): 19–28.

Reighart, Renee, and Cyril Oberlander. 2008. Exploring the future of interlibrary loan: Generalizing the experience of the University of Virginia, USA. *Interlending & Document Supply 36*(4): 184–190.

Ward, Suzanne M. 2002. Books on demand: Just-in-time acquisitions. *The Acquisitions Librarian 27*: 95–107.

Ward, Suzanne M., Tanner Wray, and Karl Debus-Lopez. 2003. Collection development based on patron requests: Collaboration between interlibrary loan and acquisitions. *Library Collections, Acquisitions, & Technical Services 27*: 203–213.

APPENDIX: GIST ACQUISITIONS WORKFLOW MAP

Want Buy-In? Let Your Students Do the Buying! A Case Study of Course-Integrated Collection Development

ANNE C. BARNHART

University of California, Santa Barbara, California

This paper describes how library instruction sessions (both one-shots and credit-bearing information literacy courses) can be used as collection development opportunities. Students were assigned the project of selecting materials for the library's collection as a way to demonstrate understanding of research tools. The titles selected by the students were purchased by the library. The author discusses the creation of this assignment and how it served to increase course enrollment and build a more useful library collection. This model integrates outreach efforts with collection building and information literacy.

Whenever librarians have consistent interaction with researchers, whether at the reference desk, in the classroom, or in office hours, they learn what resources those users need. By helping patrons with interlibrary loan requests, librarians see what kinds of resources are lacking in the present collection. Through assisting students with in-depth research questions, the librarians' radars become tuned in to other resources the students might want. Frequent interactions with users help subject specialists in collection development in myriad conscious and unconscious ways by making a title seem more attractive when seen in a publisher catalog or by associating a specific author with a specific graduate student's research. This practice is fairly well accepted by librarians as the norm. At the University of California, Santa

Barbara (UCSB), I decided to merge this concept with my library instruction classes.

The library instruction program at UCSB is quite extensive. In addition to the typical one-hour bibliographic instruction sessions, UCSB has credit-bearing courses on library research methodology. There is a lower-level course for one credit hour and an upper-level course worth two credit hours. The upper-level course had extremely low enrollment, probably partly due to its name: Advanced Library Bibliography. As the librarian for Religious Studies, Chicana/o Studies, and Latin American & Iberian Studies at UCSB from 2005 to 2009, I redesigned the upper-level course and made discipline-specific sections: Advanced Library Research for Latin American, Iberian and Chicana/o Studies; and Advanced Library Research for Religious Studies. The courses were aimed at both upper-division undergraduates and grad-uate students. The Latin American, Iberian, and Chicana/o Studies course attracted both undergraduates and graduate students. The Religious Stud-ies section, however, was solely taken by graduate students. These courses were designed to teach students how to approach library research in these interdisciplinary fields. Students were strongly encouraged to be concurrently enrolled in a course with a research requirement so they could use the library course as a laboratory to do their work for the other class. The first iteration of the course had a fairly typical and uninspired final project: an annotated bibliography of the materials students had identified throughout the quarter. This project was very similar to the assignment given in the lower-level library research class. A problem with this final project arose if another course in which the student was enrolled required an annotated bibliography as part of its research project. One of the definitions of cheating at UCSB is "submitting substantial portions of the same academic work for credit in more than one course without consulting with the second instructor (and the first instructor if the courses are concurrent at UCSB)" (University of California). While it is not likely that a professor would object to a bibliography being assigned in a library course, keeping this assignment did entail a certain amount of risk.

There were other problems with the advanced library research courses. While the courses were well-received and highly recommended by faculty members to their students, at only two credit hours and fulfilling only elec-tive requirements, the courses were not inherently appealing to students. Students who did take the courses gave extremely positive feedback, and word of mouth boosted enrollment to some extent. Incoming graduate stu-dents were strongly encouraged to take the courses, but most of these same students already felt overwhelmed by their regular course load and, in some cases, by new teaching responsibilities. UCSB also has a policy that graduate students can drop a class without penalty on the last day of instruction for that term. As a result, several graduate students put off doing the assignments and then dropped the course during the last week without having done any work. While the librarian was glad to have taught these students how to do research, the cold reality is that the library also needed those final enrollment statistics to justify continuing to offer the course. The course needed a way to inspire graduate students to stay through the end of the semester and complete the coursework. It needed a new final project that would serve to showcase what the students had learned throughout the course and to give them an incentive to complete the course, but not be an assignment that would be duplicated in another course.

The new final project I created required the students to demonstrate the following: understanding of the literature in their field; ability to search through local, consortial, and national library catalogs; familiarity with article databases for locating book reviews; and mastery of citation searching. It also provided motivation for students to enroll in the course and complete the work because they would receive something tangible for their work. For the new final project, the students selected books for the library's collection. I "gave" each them a specific dollar amount from my funds (initially $350), and they had to determine how the money would be spent. At the end of the quarter, I submitted orders for the items the students had identified, putting "notify" notes in the order records so they would be the first patrons to use the materials they selected. The orders were only submitted upon completion of the course, so students dropping the course at the last minute would, in theory, not have their materials purchased.

The selection assignment had certain rules attached to it as part of the requirements and the grading scheme. Students were given a dollar amount, and they had to spend the entire amount within 5%. They were allowed to pool their funds with someone else in the class if they had shared interests. If the student recommended a book that UCSB already owned, not only would the student lose that money but there was also a corresponding reduction of the grade since the student had not properly searched the library catalog. If a title the student recommended was already held by several campuses in the University of California system, the student had to justify why UCSB should duplicate content. I was very liberal in evaluating the justification students used for duplicating a title already held in the University of California system. The Religious Studies department at UCSB is the flagship program in the system and, sometimes, Religious Studies students believed that UCSB should have certain titles because they are standards in the field. These students were encouraged to use citation searches or book reviews in academic publications to justify system-wide duplication of a title. A few students wanted to add another copy of some titles because they believed the books to be a key part of their doctoral research projects and did not want to be constantly borrowing the books through interlibrary loan. All of these could be valid reasons for duplicating content within our consortium, but the students had to defend their decisions.

Students were also instructed on the realities of interlibrary loan and library budgets and told to consider format in making their selection decisions. Since videos are typically much harder to get through interlibrary loan than books, many students gave priority to media. For some topics, videos were the primary format for materials. Of course, students were also interested in journal subscriptions and databases. Unfortunately, UCSB could not commit to any ongoing expenses, so new subscriptions and licenses were not options for this assignment. One student, however, identified a back-run of a specific Buddhist studies journal and, since it was a back-run, it was an acceptable one-time expense.

This assignment allowed students to create the collection that they were going to need for their doctoral research. Student response to this assignment was overwhelmingly positive. At first they were a little incredulous: "You are actually going to buy the things I pick?" was a common reaction. Students would encourage other students to enroll in the course because of the final book-buying project. One quarter, on the first day of class, I was explaining the syllabus and the assignments, and when I got to the final project, one student said to another, "I heard about this from a second-year student! This is so cool!" I knew then that I had created an assignment that was a great marketing tool.

The final assignment had another practical application for the students, and I explained this to them as well. Many of the students who graduate from UCSB accept teaching positions at smaller colleges that do not have subject specialists in the libraries. These students are going to be faculty library liaisons and will find themselves sending purchase requests to the library (often even providing a vendor catalog or supplier for international materials) in order to obtain the books they want in their campus library. The final assignment introduced them to some of the tools of the trade for selecting books and presented some of the limitations of library budgets, for example, one time purchase versus ongoing expenditure. It also showed them how they could more successfully collaborate with their colleagues and lobby the library to purchase expensive material. I was not trying to turn future professors into collection development librarians, but to arm them with the knowledge they will need when they find book selection on their list of faculty responsibilities in their first teaching position.

The book-buying final project was not without its complications. One of the first hurdles I experienced was my colleagues' reactions. Some librarians did not approve of the assignment and tried to use it as evidence that my collections were over-funded, since, obviously, I had too much money if I was going to let random students spend it how they wished. The irony of that argument was, of course, that nearly all collection development librarians make purchases based on graduate student and faculty requests. I was only marketing this standard procedure and using it in a class.

Thankfully, that reaction was not shared by the majority of my colleagues or by the library administration at UCSB. Other colleagues expressed concern that I was trying to teach graduate students how to do professional librarians' work. Many of these colleagues did not have experience at smaller institutions and were surprised to learn that faculty at smaller colleges often make selection decisions for the library. I also was careful to make sure that the departments did not think I was trying to train the graduate students to become librarians. Students were not allowed to use *Choice* or other librarian tools for the book reviews since the goal was for them to be learning the tools of their field, not how to be a librarian. Nevertheless, students who had taken one of the advanced research courses were often subsequently employed by the library as student assistants.

The timing of the courses was also tricky. The Religious Studies department recommended that the course be taught in the fall quarter when graduate students were new to campus. My original intent for the course was to help the Religious Studies students complete their master's theses, so my goal for the course was to attract students at a later point in their academic careers. Further, I was concerned that incoming students were too overwhelmed by the reality of graduate school to be able to make the most of the course. However, I was very happy to have the support of the Religious Studies faculty for the course, so I accommodated their timing request. The chair also encouraged students to take the course by making it count for one of the mandatory "departmental colloquium" credit hours. The Latin American & Iberian Studies department wanted their section to be taught in the spring quarter so the students could gain the research background just prior to having a summer dedicated to research for their senior honors or master's theses. The problem with this timing was that spring quarter starts in April and our book ordering ends in the last week of March. When the final project was just an annotated bibliography, spring quarter worked well. However, when the project changed to book selection, I would have had to delay purchasing the students' selections until the following fiscal year. Officially, the fiscal year started in July, but due to California's budgetary quirks, the book budget was not available until late September or October. I wanted the students to be able to get more immediate gratification, so I moved the Latin American, Iberian, and Chicana/o Studies section to winter quarter, which ends in mid-March, but this solution did not work as well for the department's goals.

The most significant problem I encountered was the inconsistency of the amount of money each student was allowed to spend. With the ever-decreasing California state budget, I had less money from my collections funds to dedicate to this purpose. Also, with the increasing enrollment in the course, that smaller account balance had to be split among more students. New students, many of whom were attracted to the course because they had heard that last year's cohort spent $350 each, were given only $215 each. I think this budgetary reality severely restricts the long-term viability of this assignment for this course.

I also experimented with this kind of project outside of the confines of the credit-bearing course. As the librarian for Latin American & Iberian Studies, I was also the liaison to the Department of Spanish and Portuguese. Those graduate students did not enroll in my library research course since their department had its own mandatory research methodology seminar taken by all students. Working with the professors of that seminar, I was able to add the book selection project as an assignment. These students, like the ones in the credit-bearing courses, were very excited about the prospect of being able to spend the library's money and were pleased when the items they had selected were finally received. The faculty members were pleased that the students were creating a useful research collection for their doctoral work. Through the Spanish and Portuguese student exercise, I was able to see a tangible shift in the interest of our incoming students and a glaring disconnect between their interests and our previous approval plan profiles. While our faculty had more traditional research interests that had been driving our book selection, I saw that the students were increasingly interested in the intersection of literature and film. The graduate students in Spanish and Portuguese were selecting books about the director Almodóvar, Mexican film noir, and film adaptations of literature. I was not aware of this trend, and later, when I went to the book fairs in Guadalajara and Buenos Aires, I had a better grasp of what UCSB students wanted. For years, I had done the traditional meet-and-greet with incoming students, encouraging them to let me know their research interests, but this approach was not nearly as effective as assigning them each a budgetary amount and saying, "Spend it!" Not only did I buy the specific titles they chose, but I also had a much greater understanding of the kinds of materials to select when I reviewed publisher catalogs or displays.

As indicated above, budgetary problems might threaten the future of this kind of patron-initiated collection development. However, with ever-shrinking collections budgets, libraries are also less able to build collections that are just-in-case. Having graduate students systematically create the collections they know they will need allows librarians to anticipate what users will want. Shifting some funds from established approval plans to student-initiated selection projects would create a more useful collection while also demonstrating the library's responsiveness to scholars.

As a form of outreach, the course-integrated collection development method connects students to the collection in a very tangible manner. It helps tailor part of the collection to the ones who will be its heaviest users for the next five or seven years. It also creates user satisfaction and serves as a feel-good marketing tool in a time when library service and customer satisfaction are becoming increasingly important for our very survival.

REFERENCE

University of California, Santa Barbara. Office of Judicial Affairs. *Academic Integrity at UCSB: A Student's Guide.* http://judicialaffairs.sa.ucsb.edu/pdf/academicintegflyer.pdf (accessed April 11, 2010).

User-Driven Acquisitions: Allowing Patron Requests to Drive Collection Development in an Academic Library

LESLIE J. REYNOLDS, CARMELITA PICKETT,
WYOMA VANDUINKERKEN, JANE SMITH, JEANNE HARRELL,
and SANDRA TUCKER

Texas A&M University, College Station, Texas

In 2007 Texas A&M University (TAMU) Libraries adopted an approach to monograph collection development that uses an unconventional fund structure and sets aside funds for user requests, called Suggest a Purchase. After initiating this change, the libraries realized that its patrons had become actively engaged in selecting materials for the collection. Data will be presented describing user and librarian levels of satisfaction with the Suggest a Purchase program. Additional data will be presented describing what was requested, what was ordered, how much the materials circulated, who requested materials, and the increase in requests over time.

INTRODUCTION

Since the mid-1990s, subject specialist librarians at Texas A&M University (TAMU) Libraries have been responsible for making monographic selection decisions (both electronic and print) for the library collection. Although most of these librarians have advanced degrees in their subject area and work closely with their assigned groups, the use of the print collection has gone down over time. This trend is found in most academic libraries across the United States, where it is estimated that many monographs in a typical academic library collection never circulate (Kent 1979). In an attempt to reverse this trend by involving patrons in collection development efforts,

TAMU Libraries adopted an approach that uses an unconventional fund structure and sets aside funds for items requested by users through its Suggest a Purchase program. In evaluating the program, the libraries discovered that its patrons became actively engaged in selecting materials for the collection (vanDuinkerken et al. 2008, 142–149). Many of the users of the service reported increased use of the library. In this article, the authors present data describing user and librarian levels of satisfaction with the Suggest a Purchase program and additional data outlining what was requested, what was ordered, how much the materials circulated, who requested materials, and the increase in requests over time.

USER-DRIVEN ACQUISITIONS AT TAMU

TAMU has purchased monographs requested through interlibrary loan since the late 1990s and has featured a Suggest a Purchase form on its library Web site for several years. In 2006 the TAMU Libraries decided to expand its user-driven acquisitions program in conjunction with an effort to simplify its acquisitions fund structure. At that time, the TAMU Libraries' acquisitions budget contained 237 monographic fund lines: 31 approval fund lines and 206 firm order fund lines. As there was only one source for the 31 approval fund lines, it made sense to consolidate them. Of the remaining 206 funds, 75 could be eliminated immediately since they were allocated zero dollar amounts and were therefore never used, and nine other fund lines could be eliminated because they were earmarked for summer spending. Six restricted endowment fund lines needed to be retained. The remaining subject-specific fund lines had traditionally been assigned to individual subject librarians (vanDuinkerken et al. 2008). In fiscal year 2007, the collection development management team collapsed the approval funds and the individual subject-specific funds into five unrestricted fund lines that could be used for one-time purchases of monographic materials in print, electronic, or other media formats. These were defined as:

- The approval fund, used to purchase materials supplied through the library's principal approval vendor—whether through the approval plan or a firm order (55% of monographic budget).
- The user-generated fund, used to purchase materials requested by a university student, staff, or faculty member (6% of monographic budget).
- The library-generated fund, used to purchase materials selected by a librarian that total up to $1,000 (5% of monographic budget).
- The library proposal fund, used to purchase materials selected by a user or a librarian that cost more than the threshold price of $1,000 and less than the big ticket threshold of $10,000. Additionally, a proposal to purchase more than 25 related items at one time or over a short period of time requires the use of this fund (4% of monographic budget).

- The big ticket fund, used to fund "one-time cost" materials selected by a user or a librarian that are priced over the threshold of $10,000 (30%) of monographic budget.

The goals of the new fund structure are discussed in detail in the van-Duinkerken et al. (2008) paper and included the following:

- Fund the purchase of all reasonable requests from affiliated users.
- Fill all reasonable requests in a timely manner.
- Increase communication with users during the purchase process.
- Free librarians from the requirement to spend and track individual funds.
- Free librarian time for outreach to users.
- Simplify the accounting system.

Some librarians were concerned that users would select materials inappropriate for a research library and deplete available funds. Other concerns related to the time and effort involved in preparing proposals for items or groups of items costing between $1,000 and $10,000. On the positive side, selectors could see that they might have access to more funding than before. Also, they were glad to be relieved of the expectation to spend their allotted funds to meet performance expectations. These and other issues are addressed in the librarian survey results below.

With the new fund structure in place, the library now purchases all items requested by users if the item costs less than $150 and is not already owned. When a user requests an item with the Suggest a Purchase form, the library's e-mail system generates an automated response acknowledging the request and forwards the request to the monograph acquisitions unit. If the item costs more than $150, a subject librarian must approve the purchase. When the order is placed, monograph acquisitions notifies the user, with a blind copy to the appropriate librarian(s) (the subject specialist responsible for the call number range and the library liaison to the user's department). If the user has requested notification of purchase, a public-services unit contacts the user when the item is available for checkout.

Shortly after the policy of automatic purchases was implemented, librarians began promoting it during instruction sessions and in written communications with their constituents. Usage has grown steadily as reported below.

EVALUATION OF THE PROGRAM

Data for this paper were collected in two ways: surveys of users and librarians and an analysis of the user-generated purchase request forms. For the user survey, 900 e-mails were sent to patrons who requested materials using the Web-based Suggest a Purchase request form and who asked to be notified when the item was available for checkout. The libraries received 186 responses. For the librarian survey, 42 subject specialist librarians and liaisons were contacted and 25 responses were received.

The authors also examined the purchase request forms from fiscal years 2007, 2008, and 2009 (fiscal year is September to August) to analyze what was requested, what was ordered, who requested materials, and the increase in requests over time. Purchase request forms were matched with order and catalog records in the Voyager system in order to analyze circulation. Additionally, requests were tagged with a format code (book, DVD, etc.) and user status (faculty, staff, graduate, or undergraduate).

Results From the User Survey

Users were asked 14 satisfaction-driven questions with two open-ended questions requesting suggestions for improvements and general feedback. Figure 1 shows the user status percentages of the survey participants. Faculty and graduate students were the major responders; they account for 70% of the survey responses.

When asked to rate satisfaction with the Suggest a Purchase service, 97% were satisfied with the overall service; of these, 61% indicated they were very satisfied. The survey showed that 70% of the respondents increased their library usage as a result of the service. When asked to describe their level of library use, 64% said they were frequent to heavy users of the library (more than three times a week). Users were asked whether materials in general were received in the time frame expected; 90% responded positively.

The survey also revealed areas of dissatisfaction, one of which was communication regarding the fulfillment of their request. One user suggested, "... it would be helpful to receive updates along the process (i.e., we have

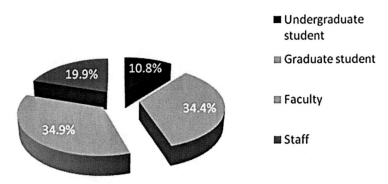

FIGURE 1 User survey response.

approved your request, we are looking for the book, the book has been ordered, the book is en route)." Such notifications would be comparable to the service received from Amazon or other online merchants. There was also frustration with the amount of time it took for materials to arrive in the library. One respondent shared, "Materials took about five to six weeks to arrive, as it was course work–related I was already half way in my semester. I would suggest the course work–related books to arrive at maximum two weeks." Users were asked whether any of their purchase requests had been denied; 17% indicated that they were unsure. Several users commented in the survey that their requests were denied and they did not know why, as no one had communicated this information to them. When users were asked specifically whether they were contacted by the library with questions or concerns related to purchase requests, 36% indicated that they had been contacted. Additionally, when asked whether they had received notification that their items had arrived, 7% said no.

Other useful data were also gleaned from the user survey, such as how often patrons used the service and the purpose of the request. Based on the survey results, 79% of the respondents used the Suggest a Purchase service more than once, including 5% who used it more than 25 times. Users were asked to indicate the format of material requested; 87% indicated print while 38% indicated video or DVD. Users were also asked to identify the purposes related to their requests for materials; research not related to a course was the most frequent response at 61%, with recreation the second most frequent response at 29.9% (Figure 2). From the data collected through the Suggest a Purchase forms, librarians determined that the major users of the Suggest a Purchase service are faculty members and graduate students. The user survey revealed that the majority of requests were for research purposes, rather than for course work. Overall, users are very satisfied with the service, and most used it more than once. Users identified communication as their only area of dissatisfaction; they would like more information about the progress of each request.

Results From the Librarian Survey

In 2007, when the new user-driven acquisition policy was presented to subject specialists, several advantages were highlighted: 237 funds were consolidated into five funds (not counting restricted gift funds) so less subject specialist effort and time was needed to code and track funds; additional time for subject specialists to evaluate the collection; more meaningful information on collection and funding trends; increased opportunities for communicating with users about collection needs; as well as visible demonstration that the TAMU Libraries trusted its users to choose information resources wisely. Subject specialist reactions to the fund structure change were mixed. Some

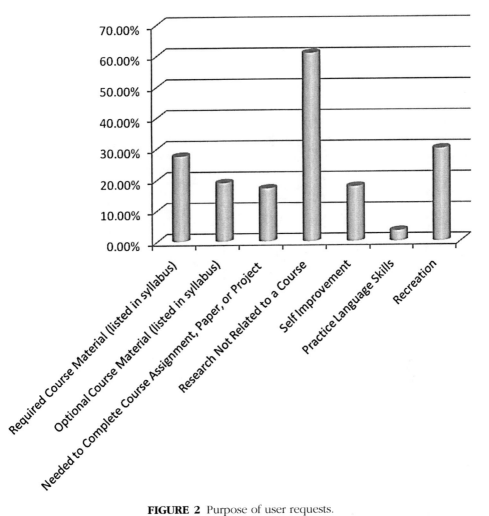

FIGURE 2 Purpose of user requests.

subject specialists were concerned that users, rather than subject specialists, would be directing collection development and that the users would spend the entire monographic budget before subject specialists had sufficient time to identify needed materials. Subject specialists were also concerned that users would request inappropriate materials without subject specialist input.

Forty-two subject specialist librarians and liaisons were asked to complete an 11-question survey to gauge the perceived effectiveness and satisfaction with policy and procedural changes. A Likert scale was designed to allow librarians to rate their level of satisfaction related to this service. All questions included opportunities for free-form feedback. Twenty-five librarians (60%) responded to this request. Over half (52%) of the respondents were initially concerned that users would select inappropriate materials for a research library (i.e., selecting non-scholarly items). Another initial

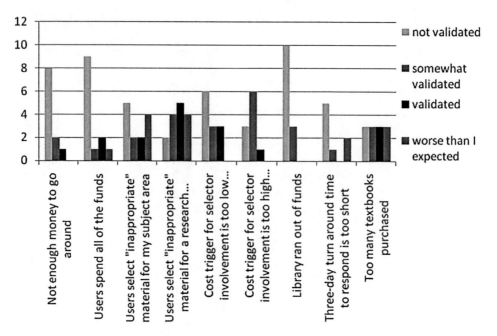

FIGURE 3 Librarians' initial concerns.

concern noted by 47% of the respondents was that a large number of textbooks would be purchased. Librarians were asked whether their initial concerns were validated after implementation of this policy. Forty-five percent of the librarians said that their concern that users would spend all the money was not validated, while 35% had not been concerned with this possibility at all. Even though users spent less than the budget earmarked for their requests, 20% of the librarians indicated that this concern was somewhat validated and one even indicated that it was worse than expected (Figure 3).

When asked to comment on user requests aligning with current collection development policy, 62.5% of the librarians agreed that most requests had aligned; 37.5% stated that few of the requests were aligned. Eighty-eight percent said that they have not needed to adjust their collection development policies in response to users' needs. One of those who did make changes as a result of information gleaned from user requests stated, "In my CD [policy] I made sure to look at videos, as this is one of the most requested formats." Overall satisfaction with the Suggest a Purchase service was fairly high. Eighty percent of the librarians were satisfied or very satisfied with the policy to purchase items under $150, the process in place to make these purchases, as well as the communications about these requests with their users.

One of the goals of the program was to increase communication. As for communications between librarians and the acquisitions unit, 84% were satisfied or very satisfied. The only concern noted was that the subject specialist was not notified unless the request was over $150. This comment demonstrates a breakdown in communications as all related subject specialists and departmental liaisons are supposed to be notified of every user request regardless of cost. The new model requires direct communication between subject specialists and users for items over $150, for multiple requests, or for questions regarding the request. Thirty-three percent of the subject specialists contacted users because the cost of the item was too high, and 25% contacted users because they had requested an item already owned by the libraries. Several of the librarians made contact with the users to discuss format availability or edition desired. One librarian commented, "I contacted a few requestors because they were faculty and [I] wanted to offer my services. I contacted another to let him know why I turned down his request and offered alternatives." A majority of the librarians polled (71%) stated that the Suggest a Purchase service improved their knowledge of their users' areas of study and research. Eighty-seven percent agreed that the service has been well-received by their user groups. One librarian recommended that there be a "Suggest another item" option at the bottom of the page so that users could submit more than one item without having to reenter their personal information, a comment echoed in the user survey.

Analysis of User-Generated Purchase Request Forms

The TAMU Libraries received a total of 13,121 Suggest a Purchase requests. Of these requests, a total of 9,825 (75%) items were added to the collection: 8,665 from the user-generated fund and 1,160 from the approval fund. Staff did not order 2,767 items, either because they were already owned (1,981 or 15% of the titles) or because they were not yet published (786 or 6% of the titles). An additional 388 (3%) requests were for journal subscriptions, which are reviewed once a year through a previously created procedure. The remaining 141 (1%) requests were forwarded to the Medical Science Library for review and purchase. The procedure calls for users to be notified to let them know whether their requests were ordered; for materials requested that were already owned by the library, the individual was told how to find them.

The number of requests submitted through the Suggest a Purchase request form increased over time. During the 2007 fiscal year (September 2006 through August 31, 2007), there were 2,495 requests. In the 2008 fiscal year, the number of requests increased by 2% to 2,544, followed by a 43% increase in 2009 to 3,626 requests.

Based on the figures retrieved from the purchase request forms, the breakdown by user status was 44% from faculty, 27% from graduate students, 19% from undergraduates, and 9% from staff affiliated with the university (Figure 4).

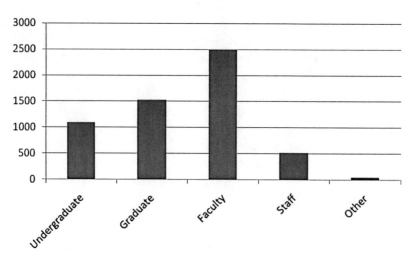

FIGURE 4 User requests by category of requestor.

The Suggest a Purchase form included a field requesting department affiliation. Although it was not always filled with a meaningful designation, the researchers were able to identify participation by 134 different departments. The largest percentage of requests came from the Arts and Humanities departments followed by requests from Social Sciences and Engineering. The large volume of requests from Arts and Humanities is not surprising in that TAMU is historically a land grant institution originally grounded in the sciences. The collections in Humanities and Social Sciences are less developed.

Table 1 illustrates the various formats of the 9,825 items purchased as the result of user-driven acquisitions. The data show that the most common format requested was print, followed by DVDs. The data indicate that the majority of the DVD requests came from faculty members.

The researchers found quite interesting results in the circulation statistics for the 8,665 titles purchased from the user-generated fund. Nearly 78% of

TABLE 1 User Requests by Format

Format	Number of Titles	Percentage of Total
Print	6,213	63.24%
DVD	3,210	32.67%
Audio CD	165	1.68%
Music CD	140	1.43%
Electronic Book	70	0.71%
VHS	13	0.13%
CD-Roms	13	0.13%
Microtext	1	0.01%
Total	9,825	100%

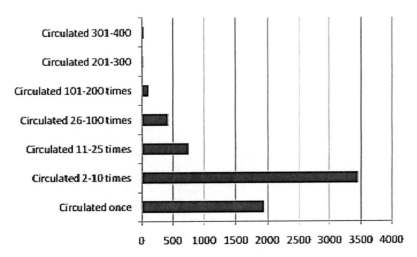

FIGURE 5 Circulation of total number of requested titles.

the titles circulated during the three-year period. Nearly 40% of the total titles circulated more than once. One title circulated 430 times, a title on course reserve (Figure 5).

CONCLUSION

To summarize, there were 13,121 Suggest a Purchase requests during the three-year period covered by the study. Of the 8,665 user-generated fund requests, 78% circulated during the three years. Most of the requests came from faculty and graduate students who needed the materials for research rather than course work. Users requested primarily print followed by DVDs. Based on the user survey, 97% were satisfied with the overall service. Many users expressed delight that the library offers this service and hope it continues. When asked to describe satisfaction with aspects of the service users identified satisfaction that the correct item was purchased (99%) and that it was delivered to the correct location (95%). One area identified for improvement was communication between the library and users regarding the process from original request to item delivery and every step in between.

According to the librarian survey, initial concerns were focused on the appropriateness of the material requested and the potential for users to spend a disproportionate share of the funds. When asked whether these concerns were validated three years after implementation, a majority of the librarians who responded to the question about a possible shortage of funds said no. Some librarians (20%) continue to be concerned about the appropriateness of the material requested by users. This concern might be alleviated by the comment of a user who said, "I feel obliged to keep up with the latest in my field, even outside of my immediate research area—for my teaching, and because curiosity of students begins with curiosity of teachers."

The results show that this model of user-driven acquisitions is valued by users at all levels of the university community. As stated in an enthusiastic comment on the survey:

> This is a fantastic system/policy and, in my opinion, a major selling point of TAMU to prospective faculty and students (especially graduate students). In recruitment efforts I have actively called attention to your ability and willingness to continue developing the collection according to patrons' needs even in tight budgetary times; this really sets TAMU apart from many peer institutions. I applaud the library for being so responsive to faculty and student needs: without such responsiveness, our research and teaching, both central to the work we do here, would encounter many more obstacles than it does.

REFERENCES

Kent, Allen. 1979. *Use of library materials: The University of Pittsburgh study.* New York: M. Dekker.

vanDuinkerken, Wyoma, Jane Smith, Jeanne Harrell, Leslie J. Reynolds, Sandra Tucker, and Esther Carrigan. 2008. Creating a flexible fund structure to meet the needs and goals of the library and its users. *Library Collections, Acquisitions, and Technical Services 32*(3/4): 142–149.

Some Thoughts on Opportunities for Collection Development Librarians

MARIANNE STOWELL BRACKE, JEAN-PIERRE V. M. HÉRUBEL
and SUZANNE M. WARD

Purdue University, West Lafayette, Indiana

New and emerging roles are transforming the landscape of academic librarianship. This paper focuses on the changes facing academic librarians whose activities and responsibilities in collections are shifting, particularly in the face of greater emphasis on user-driven collection development. Librarians' reduced role in routine collection development translates into gaining more time and support to move in other directions. Among many exciting and interesting opportunities, librarians apply their subject expertise in such strategic initiatives as information literacy, research, e-science, digital humanities projects, and collaborative print retention efforts. They can also participate more in campus affairs.

INTRODUCTION

Librarians everywhere grapple with change these days. It is not just technology that has changed both the nature of many aspects of our jobs as well as the way we do them. A kaleidoscope of events contributes to a professional landscape that looks very different than it did even five years ago:

- Changing user needs and expectations
- Growing user interest in self-service models
- Changing needs for designing and allocating library space
- Economic crisis in terms of reduced purchasing power, stagnant salaries, furloughs, layoffs, and unfilled vacant positions

- New knowledge and skills that librarians can and should embrace
- The imminent wave of retirees with fewer new colleagues to replace them
- Managing emerging formats while simultaneously maintaining and supporting traditional formats

These changes affect all areas of librarianship. However, this paper examines the effect of these changes on academic collection development librarians from the synthesized experiences of the authors at a large research university, especially as it relates to patron-driven selection models replacing a portion of the expert selector tradition. Some librarians view these impending changes with trepidation; this paper postulates that rather than creating a threatening environment, these changes presage a new era of opportunity.

Perhaps nervous collection development librarians remember the situation about two decades ago when the widespread availability first of indexes on CD-ROM and then of online databases slowly eclipsed and then eliminated the need for mediated database searches. This cycle of decline eliminated a service that engaged some librarians nearly full time and others for a portion of their time. A better parallel could be drawn from the realm of cataloging. Every library once had a group of catalogers creating original records for items that did not have DLC cataloging. Then came OCLC, which allowed easier and quicker shared cataloging. Trained staff could now handle the routine aspects of cataloging, freeing time for librarian catalogers to focus their expertise on new areas or on unusual situations that required a specialized degree of knowledge. Although automation and sharing of some basic aspects of cataloging eliminated the need for so many catalogers, it opened up new opportunities that took better advantage of their specialized knowledge and skills.

Should selectors, especially those with full-time collection development responsibilities, fear the same outcome accelerated by a proliferation of patron-initiated selection plans? On the contrary, the authors believe that a reduced role in routine collection development opens up an exciting new range of potential roles that also require the subject librarian's expertise, insight, and experience.

NEW ROLES

Librarians' new collection development roles may be an extension of existing tasks, or they might allow for more time to be spent engaging in new or emerging roles in librarianship. They also suggest a range of roles—not all performed by any one individual, but merged into current responsibilities or exchanged for dwindling or defunct responsibilities. Patron-initiated selection plans have been established as a successful way to supplement current collection development strategies, as the articles in this issue document.

Combining this strategy with other tools, such as approval plans and shelf-ready books, collection development librarians spend less time identifying and selecting current titles of immediate interest to their population. Librarians can now focus their skills on higher-level tasks to support the changing needs of students and faculty.

Collection management will continue to be an activity in need of librarian expertise. Librarians are responsible for building useful, coherent collections that fulfill both current user needs and anticipate the needs of future generations. There will be a need to spend time in emerging areas, such as exploring e-data potential for collections, or in expanding current responsibilities. For instance, management of the physical collection will continue to be an issue. Space-driven concerns will increase the need for cooperative collection building and resource sharing, management of print deselection projects, and exploration of cooperative print retention programs. Librarians can capitalize on their strengths through deeper and more sophisticated analysis of collection use data. They can turn their attention to licensing electronic resources and creating and managing digital collections. Finally, librarians will need to explore new or improved collection models, for instance, by enhancing user-driven collection methods, by improving the balance between approval plans and expert selection, or by developing pay-per-view models for content.

Other roles may fall outside collection management but be an outgrowth of subject specialty. Librarians can develop deeper, more meaningful relationships with faculty and instructors as liaisons to academic departments. These closer relationships may result in two major areas of opportunity. The first is information literacy, which could take the form of institution-wide programs, embedded librarians in classroom settings, outreach to distance students, or consulting hours outside of the library in areas where students congregate. Librarians can also take the lead in teaching specialized tools, such as *EndNote*.

The second major area of opportunity is less traditional and involves partnering with researchers at earlier stages of their research. Generally, librarians interact with research as a finished product: a document, a book, a data set, etc. There are now opportunities, however, for librarians to become part of the research process further upstream, where research begins. As researchers embark on new projects, they need to establish a program for managing their data: creating, identifying, sharing, and storing. Librarians can partner with researchers to design data management systems, with the librarians being responsible for data curation and metadata creation.

Librarians may also expand their involvement in a host of other roles. For example, scholarly communication is an area that is rich in opportunity. Activities include educating authors on copyright, becoming advocates of open access, taking on the role of online publisher, and generally campaigning for reform in current publishing models. Revenue-generating roles, such as grant writing and donor relations, may also be a possibility. Librarians can also play a larger role in developing the next generation of librarians through mentoring staff or junior colleagues, developing more internships for library school students, and participating in diversity programs.

Another option for librarians, especially those in tenure-track positions, is the avenue of research enhancement. No longer need librarians lament over not having enough time and infrastructural support; their changing role may permit time for reflection, generating research problems, and sharing research ideas and attendant approaches and methodologies, thus leading to the creation of a sustainable research environment and culture. In these difficult economic times, it is easy to become wholly engaged with the day-to-day tasks, but it is equally important to reserve a portion of the directional energy to focus on thinking about and planning for the future. Practicing librarians who are actively and demonstrably engaged in the discovery of knowledge that adds to the library and information science research domain would offer even more value to the profession. Another golden opportunity is the linkage of librarians engaged in research and disciplinary faculty, wherever collaboration is desirable and shared expertise can lead to joint ventures in research and eventual publication. Beyond these examples, librarians can move into ventures where sponsored research in a disciplinary department requires library and information science expertise vis-à-vis data stream or e-data stewardship.

Perhaps last, but not least in importance, are governance roles that librarians may take on once released from routine tasks. University and collegiate communities function via committee and team efforts. On some campuses, librarians enjoy such privileges as participating on the committees responsible for the maintenance and smooth running of campus life. Librarians bring a unique perspective to the faculty senate and to committees on everything from infrastructure to information literacy, groundskeeping, and building maintenance. In the past, librarians may not always have been perceived as possible candidates for inclusion on these committees, but if librarians have more time to offer their expertise and their unique library and information science perspective they will be acknowledged for their contributions outside library matters.

CONCLUSION

Change is inevitable. Librarians can decide to wait for change and adapt, however painfully, when it is no longer possible to maintain old ways. The authors advocate the alternative: seizing the new opportunities that change brings or, better yet, pioneering and creating some of those opportunities. While old, comfortable routines may be missed, there are many equally fulfilling and exciting contributions ahead for collection development librarians:

educating the next generation of professionals and scholars; collaborating in research opportunities; engaging more fully with the academic community; exploring new technology; and exercising subject knowledge and expertise to create and manage the library collections of the future.

FURTHER READING

Alsop, Justine, and Karen Bordonaro. 2007. Multiple roles of academic librarians. *E-JASL: Electronic Journal of Academic and Special Librarianship* 8(1). http://southernlibrarianship.icaap.org/content/v08n01/alsop_j01.htm.

Cipkin, Christopher, and David Stacey. 2009. Reflecting roles: Being a successful subject liaison librarian in a changing environment. *SCONUL Focus 45*: 27–30. http://www.sconul.ac.uk/publications/newsletter/45/8.pdf.

Hahn, Karla. 2009. Liaison librarian roles. *Research Library Issues: A Bimonthly Report from ARL, CNI, and SPARC 265*: 3–8. http://www.arl.org/bm˜doc/rli-265.pdf.

Hardy, Georgina, and Sheila Corrall. 2007. Revisiting the subject librarian: A study of English, law and chemistry. *Journal of Librarianship and Information Science* 30(2): 79–91.

Luca, Jonathan, and Frank Quick. 2009. The changing nature of subject liaison at St Mary's University College, Twickenham. *SCONUL Focus 45*: 24–26. http://www.sconul.ac.uk/publications/newsletter/45/7.pdf.

Williams, Karen. 2010. *Transforming Liaison Roles*. Washington, DC: Association of Research Libraries. (forthcoming).

Index